medical readings on heroin

oliver e. byrd, stanford university (emeritus)
thomas r. byrd, de anza college

boyd & fraser publishing company
san francisco, california

This book is in the
BOYD & FRASER MEDICAL READINGS SERIES

Library of Congress Catalog Number: 72-182679
ISBN: 0-87835-040-3
1 2 3 ● 4 3 2

preface

Addiction to the opiates is an ancient world problem. Heroin appears to be the most addictive of the drugs derived from opium. The use of this synthetic drug by the medical profession has been outlawed for some years. In recent years, however, the illicit use of heroin has been increased substantially according to some estimates. It is difficult to tell the magnitude of heroin addiction in the United States but there is evidence that in some communities it is substantially greater than has been previously realized.

It is likely that the use of heroin stems primarily from the inadequate personality of the addict himself, although cultural, sociological, medical, occupational and other factors may be contributing forces. The medical and paramedical sciences contain inherent occupational hazards because of closeness to the use of narcotics for the relief of pain and suffering. There are some differences in categories of addiction but consistent patterns of personality differences can be found in all.

The detection and diagnosis of narcotics addiction is often not a simple matter. The heroin addict who receives his drug is apt to be at peace with the world until his need for his next injection of the drug leads to antisocial behaviors in the ceaseless quest for the relief from distress that only the next supply of drugs can relieve.

There are multiple undesirable effects from the use of heroin, some of which are indirect and related to other behaviors. The multiple use of drugs, infections caused by the lack of hygienic measures, the addiction of babies before birth and the fatal consequences of heroin overdosage are only some of the hazards associated with this drug.

Because of the cost of illicit heroin and the fact that its sale is illegal, the average addict is driven into a life of crime.

In the past the treatment of heroin addiction has been characterized by almost constant failures. The emergence of the methadone treatment plan does not result in the cure of a narcotics addict. Methadone itself is a powerful narcotic but with many addicts it can be used as a substitute for heroin at modest cost, and some hope that the addict can be helped to abandon his life of crime for that of work or schooling and family revival.

Any community that is confronted with a heroin usage problem has multiple associated difficulties. Only a coordinated community program is likely to be successful in efforts to reduce or eliminate the problem. A fundamental question may never be solved. This question is, can society change or protect the personality of the individual who is likely to become a narcotics addict if he has the opportunity? Certain it is from the viewpoint of a stable society that the effort must be made.

O.E.B.
T.R.B.

contents

1

prevalence and significance

No one knows for certain just how extensive the use of heroin is in the United States, but all authorities, as well as addicts themselves, contend that addiction to this drug has grown tremendously in the past 15 years and that its use is greater than suspected. Evidence obtained from medical reports, hospital admissions, police records, probation reports, death rates of heroin users, and other sources do give support to the conclusion that the use of heroin has increased in this country even though the users of the drug are still a small minority of the total population.

As long ago as 1956 the first Congressionally-approved nationwide study of narcotic addiction in the United States revealed that, in the judgment of the investigators, this country had more narcotic addicts, both in numbers and percentage, than any other nation in the Western world.

It is truly impossible to say with certainty what the ultimate effect upon the total society will be, but there is evidence of present associations of crime, unemployment, family disruption, sickness and death with the use of heroin by the individual. Some psychiatrists also feel that continued drug use is a reflection of mental illness in young people, and that use of heroin assumes alarming proportions only because of the presence in our society of millions of psychotic and severely disturbed juveniles.

1

significance of continued drug abuse

in the young

Curran, Frank J. "Juveniles and Drug Abuse," New York State Journal of Medicine, 71: 1611-1622, July 1, 1971.

A consulting psychiatrist of St. Luke's Hospital in New York City, in discussing at length problems of drug abuse among young people, says that many attempts have been made to explain why the latter have turned to drugs on a large scale. Reasons given by others are the war, the draft, lack of interest in education, broken families, lack of religion, and so on.

On the other hand, the so-called normal adolescent likes and respects his parents, goes to school and college, serves time in the military, and works.

Dr. Curran says that the majority of his young patients who use drugs have been psychiatrically disturbed for years and tend to use narcotics or other drugs as a substitute for satisfactions in life that they do not find. It is this psychiatrist's conviction that the increasing use of drugs by young people is evidence of serious emotional disturbance on their parts. These disturbances have been recognized for years.

At least 10,000,000 people under the age of 25 years are thought to be suffering mental and emotional disorders, according to the final report of the Joint Commission on Mental Health of Children, and it is estimated that many are psychotic, severely disturbed, or in need of help. "These young people are crippled in their ability to learn, relate to others, to see the real world as it is, or to adequately handle their impulses of anger, fear and sex interest. They do not feel that they are a vital and effectual part of society."

It is the unstable segments of our population, according to Dr. Curran, that use drugs in an effort to solve their problems, whereas normal young people may use them out of curiosity, a desire for new experiences or because of friends. This latter group may stop the use of drugs completely or reduce their intake to a minor point. It is the psychiatrically disturbed group that continues and goes on from one drug to another. These young people should have had psychiatric care long before their first use of any drug, says the New York psychiatrist.

possible roots of addiction

Finlator, John. "The Drug Syndrome in the Affluent Society," Journal of Forensic Sciences, 13: 293–301 (No. 3), July 1968.

The Associate Director of the Bureau of Narcotics and Dangerous Drugs in Washington, D.C. observes that it is a fallacy to assume that the drug problem is new.

In an age of an affluent society we must recognize that we cannot separate the problem of drug abuse from other social phenomena of our times. Some young people suffer from boredom, an urge to defy authority, pressures from the world around them, a willingness to "try anything once," plain curiosity, and other factors that may lead them into drug abuse. Emotional or psychological difficulties, feelings of failure and inferiority, stresses beyond physical limits, and sometimes the excessive use of medicines, such as in attempts to lose body weight, may underlie the use of drugs.

Social discontent, social withdrawal and inability to compete may reflect basic underlying causes of the use of drugs, especially on the part of people who believe it is every man's right to do to his own body whatever he chooses, regardless of society. Society, however, has some responsibilities for the individual who flouts its standards, defies its laws and withdraws into a subculture, according to this narcotics official.

The overwhelming number of our young people attempt to meet the problems of an affluent society in stable, well-balanced ways, and while drug abuse may never be eliminated entirely, it is possible that better education and improved communication with each other may result in a diminished problem.

how prevalent is heroin abuse?

Alarcon, R. de, and N. H. Rathod. "Prevalence and Early Detection of Heroin Abuse," British Medical Journal, 2: 549-533, June 1, 1968.

Because the sale of heroin in the United States and European countries, as well as many others throughout the world, is illegal and punishable by severe penalties and because most users do not want their sources of supply destroyed, it is difficult to ascertain how many users of this drug exist in communities or in the nation as a whole.

Two English psychiatrists have reported on the effectiveness of five different ways of discovering heroin users in the town of Crawley. These five survey methods involved the use of information from probation officers, arrest records of the police department, medical reports from individual physicians, hospital records involving reactions to drugs and finally identification of other heroin users by addicts who have come for medical or psychiatric care. The study covered a period of two years.

Medical information on persons treated for hepatitis (inflammation of the liver) led to the discovery of 20 new heroin users, whereas identification of other users by addicts undergoing treatment revealed 46 users of the drug. Thus, of the five methods used by the English doctors, the addicts themselves proved to be the most fruitful source of discovering other heroin users, but it should be observed that the informants had experienced bad reactions from overdosage or infections; so it can be assumed that their reporting of other users had in part a desire to bring them to medical care.

Information from the police department and from probation officers was least productive in revealing new heroin users in the community. In fact, only one heroin user per 1,000 persons in the age group from 15 to 25 years was known to the authorities prior to the survey. After the study approximately 16 heroin users in the same age group had been identified.

It is likely that in any community in which one or more heroin users have been found there are many others who are not yet identified. It is also apparent that improved methods should be used for the detection of heroin users if they are to be brought to medical and psychiatric care as early as possible.

narcotic addiction and crime

Wilson, O. W. "Economic Impact of Drug Addiction," Illinois Medical Journal, 130: 522–523, October 1966.

Associations between hard narcotics and crime have been well proven. The criminal actions of addicts, however, cannot be traced solely to the use of drugs. In Chicago, for example, records show that nearly one-half of hard drug users were criminals before they began using narcotics. The same study shows, however, that the other half became involved in crime after becoming addicts. Thus, according to the Superintendent of Police in Chicago, virtually every heroin user gets involved in stealing, pushing drugs or prostitution.

Because stolen goods never bring full value when delivered to a receiver, the addict must steal about five times the amount of the sum he needs to purchase heroin. If he has a $20 per day habit he must steal $100 every day. In Chicago, at the time of this report the police had records of about 5,000 addicts. This group would have to steal about half a million dollars worth of goods every day to meet their heroin needs. The many other costs involved in narcotics control make the tax burden for the average citizen an almost staggering problem.

drugs complicate social adjustments

Goldman, Douglas. "Relationships of Social Activity, Work Capacity, Responsibility and Competence to Drug Effects," Journal of Forensic Sciences, 12: 431–443, October 1967.

A physician of Cincinnati observes that over a long period of years man has developed a high level of social organization and that drugs may have profound effects on the individual in terms of competence and responsibility in the legal sense, antisocial behavior shown by various conflicts with law and order and difficulties in industry and work situations.

The foregoing social relationships are affected because of the actions of drugs on the brain, that part of the body primarily concerned with decision making, memory, communication and performance.

All people are not equally susceptible to drugs.

It is a common experience to recognize the unfavorable actions of alcohol. Drunkenness in some persons results in hostility, combativeness, depression and minor or major deviations of conduct and thinking. Many other drugs, of which heroin is only one, affect consciousness, thinking, behavior, speed, skill and personal and work relationships. However, alcohol is the most commonly used chemical substance that adversely affects human performance and behavior, says the physician.

Narcotics such as opium, morphine, and heroin tend to produce metabolic changes in the individual and pleasurable effects that call for higher and higher dosage levels. This subjective and metabolic need for greater quantities of the drug may lead to fatal doses being self-administered by the addict.

Removal of heroin and other opiates may produce severe withdrawal symptoms which can be relieved only by more of the drugs themselves.

The addiction phenomenon is of social and legal importance because it is associated with deviant behavior, according to Doctor Goldman. Robbery, murder, the loss of social judgment and other undesirable effects of addiction to hard narcotics can be expected.

drugs for the control of pain

Aagaard, George N. "Use of Drugs in Control of Chronic Pain," Northwest Medicine, 69: 689-692 (No. 9), September 1970.

A professor of medicine at the University of Washington School of Medicine observes that there is no drug available today that is ideal for the relief of chronic, long-lasting pain. Each physician must keep three important factors in mind when he prescribes drugs for the relief of pain in a patient: 1) the severity of pain and the nature of his disease; 2) the effectiveness of the drug in relieving pain, and 3) the hazards or harmful effects of the drug. The danger of the disease must be balanced against the danger of the drug used for its treatment.

Psychological reactions almost always accompany pain. Reassurance may be a significant factor in its management.

Morphine is an ancient and valuable drug for the relief of pain. The patient is able to tolerate pain even if it still exists. The drug is a respiratory depressant and the physician must keep this fact in mind. Other complications are nausea and vomiting, constipation and low blood pressure in certain positions. Tolerance increases. Sudden relief from pain while under morphine dosage may cause severe respiratory depression. In head injuries morphine must be used with extreme caution, and also in cases where there is decreased blood volume. Persons with chronic lung disease should not be treated with morphine because of the chance of respiratory depression. Various drugs increase the adverse effects of morphine so the opiate must be used with caution in combination with other drugs. The great disadvantage of drugs such as morphine, codeine, and the analgesics such as Darvon, methadone, Demerol (meperidine) and others is that they may cause addiction.

The nature of the patient's disease may have a bearing on effectiveness of the drug. Cancer of the stomach, for example, may make it impossible for the patient to be given drugs by mouth. Liver disease may impair the metabolism of a drug. Kidney disease may restrict normal excretion of a drug and raise blood levels to the point of toxicity.

Secondary causes of pain should always be looked for and removed if possible thus decreasing the need for drug treatment. Weight reduction for an obese patient, for example, may reduce pain because of less stress on the bones and joints.

A placebo (blank) may sometimes be useful in assessing the patient's real need for pain relief. Sometimes it is wise for the doctor to start with a placebo and then proceed to the smallest effective doses that are needed for pain relief.

heroin abuse in the united states

Richards, Louise G. and Eleanor E. Carroll. "Illicit Drug Use and Addiction in the United States," Public Health Reports, 85: 1035–1041, December 1970.

Two research specialists of the Division of Narcotic Addiction and Drug Abuse of the National Institute of Mental Health observe that it is most difficult to determine how extensive the problem of drug abuse may be in the United States. Most needed statistics simply do not exist.

The only source of information on the use of illicit drugs on a national scale are from national polls, but these evaluations often use the term "ever used" or some comparable phraseology that makes it difficult to assess the findings. Other estimates on drug abuse are made from high school and college studies in scattered locations. However, at the time of this report, a national study of 50 colleges was being conducted, and other investigations of importance were under way.

The only source of national figures on "hard narcotic" addiction is from data compiled in a reporting system of the Bureau of Narcotics and Dangerous Drugs. The system depends on voluntary reports and is acknowledged to represent underestimates. Most information in this system depends on reports from law-enforcement agencies and is admittedly inadequate.

As of the beginning of 1970 the number of narcotic addicts had been put at 68,088, and more than 95 per cent of these addicts were using heroin. There were about equal numbers of whites and Negroes and more than 55 per cent were in their twenties or younger. A comparison of the number of narcotic addicts known to the Bureau of Narcotics and Dangerous Drugs for the whole state of New York with those known to New York City authorities alone in 1968 (32,240 as compared to 52,104 respectively) suggests that a more accurate estimate of the nationwide total of narcotic addicts at the beginning of 1970 would be 108,941. Most of these addicts are using heroin.

Studies of heroin-related deaths in New York City have revealed that only about one-half of 900 persons known to have died from heroin were in the city's register of narcotic addicts. From figures such as this calculations have been made that New York City alone had 104,208 users of narcotics at the beginning of 1970 and that the national total may have been more than 200,000. A serious lack of data exists on the use of narcotic drugs by adolescents.

1969 official statistics on heroin addiction challenged

Bullington, Bruce, John G. Munns, Gilbert Geis and James Raner. "Concerning Heroin Use and Official Records," American Journal of Public Health, 59: 1887–1893, October 1969.

Three narcotics research specialists and a former heroin addict observe that the accuracy and value of official statistics on heroin addiction have been received with skepticism in some quarters.

An example of major discrepancies between official estimates and those of non-official groups can be seen in the Federal Bureau of Narcotics records of 32,000 known heroin addicts in New York City as compared to the estimate of 100,000 such addicts made by the New York City Addiction Service Agency in 1968.

Many investigators believe that for every heroin addict known to enforcement agencies there is one or more unknown to police and narcotics agents.

The four investigators of this study conclude that some heroin addicts who use the drug intensively for prolonged periods may never be known to the police and that many middle-aged and medical addicts may avoid detection. They believe there is a need for more intensive effort to achieve a reliable census of heroin addicts.

Three case studies of undetected heroin addicts, 29, 34, and 36 years of age, are given in some detail by the researchers to illustrate their convictions. Although all of the three men had police records for armed robbery, assaults with deadly weapons, burglary and criminal violence, none had been identified anywhere in their records as heroin addicts.

drug abuse in an army group

Black, Samuel, Kenneth L. Owens and Ronald P. Wolff. "Patterns of Drug Use: A Study of 5,482 Subjects," American Journal of Psychiatry, 127: 420–423, October 1970.

A physician and two research associates of Fort Sill, Oklahoma have reported on the results of an anonymous questionnaire study of drug abuse in 5,482 army men. Most of the men had completed high school, but few had been to college.

Of the total group 1,497 (27 per cent) admitted having used drugs, and of those admitting their habits, 83 per cent had used marijuana, 37 per cent had taken amphetamines, 26 per cent had used LSD, and five per cent had used heroin.

The lowest incidence of drug abuse occurred in those men with the most education.

The investigators concluded that the problem of drug abuse is greater than many physicians realize and believe the explanation may lie in the fact that most doctors do not see drug users unless they are in medical difficulties of one kind or another.

Six per cent of the subjects who had used marijuana had also taken heroin. On the other hand, 97 per cent of the heroin users had also used marijuana.

If the percentage for heroin usage can be applied to the total population it would indicate that less than two-hundredths of one per cent use heroin.

heroin use multiplies by ten in the haight-ashbury

*Smith, David E., George R. Gay, Alan D. Matzger and Rose-
ann McEntee. "Pioneering Free Clinic Confronts 'New Wave'
of Heroin Epidemic," American Medical News, 13: 10-11,
December 21, 1970.*

The medical director of the Haight-Ashbury clinic of San
Francisco and his staff report that the latter city now has
about 10,000 heroin addicts and that about 50 of them visit
the clinic every day.

A special study of 435 of these heroin addicts revealed
that approximately 74 per cent were unemployed and that
about 90 per cent had used other drugs before the use of
heroin. Thirteen of the addicts began using heroin before the
age of 10 years. For the total group the daily cost of their
heroin abuse ranged from approximately $50 to $100.

Doctor Smith calls heroin the "drug of despair" and says
that it fits the pessimism of the "radical youth culture." Miss
McEntee believes that rejection of society by the young addicts lies at the roots of their addiction and that they have
chosen drugs to achieve their sociological dropout.

All members of the medical clinic urge the medical profession and hospital administrators to take constructive steps to
reverse the anti-establishment attitude of youth, through the
establishment of half-way houses, detoxification centers, hospital emergency procedures and facilities, better education of
the individual physician and better emotional and other support in the restructuring of the lifestyle of the heroin addict
who has had his first medical treatment.

infant heroin addicts in new york city

Staff. "Experts Seek Ways to Combat Neonatal Narcotics Addiction," Medical Tribune, 7: 1 ff., March 30, 1966.

Dr. Alonzo Yerby, Commissioner of Hospitals in New York City, observed in a clinical conference on narcotics addiction of newborn babies that approximately 1,000 babies a year are born addicted to heroin in that community.

Because withdrawal symptoms may not be evident for three to five days, and since many mothers leave the hospital and return home after one or two days, it is not known how many of these addicted babies die. Many of the mothers are anxious to sign out of the hospital because they fear detection and because they are also suffering withdrawal symptoms and are in a hurry to get another "fix".

Most of the children of heroin addicts are abandoned to foster care or institutions and will have all manner of psychiatric and other problems in their futures. Mrs. Katherine B. Oettinger of the Children's Bureau expressed the view that no child of a drug-addicted mother should be allowed to remain in his own home unless there is evidence that the parents are really determined to achieve their own cure.

The baby addicted to heroin usually begins to show symptoms of withdrawal about three to five days after birth. Unusual irritability, tremors, high-pitched, incessant, and shrill crying, vomiting, sneezing, respiratory distress, excessive sweating, excessive mucus secretion and failure to gain weight are some of the signs and symptoms of withdrawal from heroin on the part of the baby. Many addicted babies are premature, and prenatal care of the mother is usually poor because she avoids medical care as long as possible in order to avoid detection as a heroin addict.

From 30 to 65 per cent of the babies may be born prematurely and about 20 per cent may have some congenital defect, according to Doctor Oliver-Smith, a woman physician at the clinical conference. This physician also reports that many of the addicted mothers are prostitutes and a large proportion of the babies are illegitimate.

heroin and the law

President's Commission on Law Enforcement and Administration of Justice. Task Force Report: Narcotics and Drug Abuse. Washington, D.C.: Superintendent of Documents, 1967.

The sale or purchase of heroin in the United States is a criminal offense, observes the President's Commission. It cannot be imported or manufactured legally under any circumstances. The drug is not used in medical practice in this country.

Narcotic addiction itself is not a crime in the United States. However, addicts are prone to crime because of various reasons described below, and since the Commission estimates that there may be as many as 200,000 heroin users in this country there is a very significant criminal association between heroin and the administration of justice.

Heroin users almost invariably get involved with the police because of their constant need for the drug and because the purchase or possession of it is against the law. The sale of heroin, which is illegal, complicates life for the addict because he is apt to learn to sell the drug in order to get enough money to buy it for himself. In many states the possession of a needle or syringe for the use of heroin is also illegal, as is association of a convicted addict with other known addicts, or even to be in a place where illicit drugs are found, even if the heroin addict is genuinely unaware of the presence of such drugs. In short, the heroin addict lives in almost perpetual violation of various criminal laws. [When the possibilities of arrest for thefts, robbery and assaults are added to the foregoing hazards because of the heroin users' efforts to raise money for the purchase of the drug, it can be seen that heroin addicts are almost certain to be arrested sooner or later.—Ed.]

Drug control policies of the present century, according to the Commission, have been built around the twin judgments that drug abuse is an evil that should be suppressed and that the best way to achieve this end is by the application of criminal enforcement and penal sanctions. In keeping with this concept, federal laws have typically increased the severity of mandatory minimum terms of imprisonment for repeated offenses and at the same time making suspension of sentence, probation, or parole inapplicable to the drug offender. However, there is a broad consensus of opinion among judges and legal personnel that there are great variations in the seriousness of infractions of drug laws and that judges and correctional authorities should have the legal right to exercise discretion in the application of penalties. The President's Commission supported this latter viewpoint in its 1967 report.

heroin and federal penalties

Jerrick, Stephen J., John H. Langer, Matthew C. Resick and Sue Boe. "Current Federal Drug Laws: Explanation and Implications for Educators," Journal of School Health, 51: 459-464, November 1971.

A team of four experts has collaborated on an excellent report on current federal drug laws which is intended to assist educators in programs of drug use and drug abuse. The total report is much broader than a concern with heroin alone and should be read in full by anyone interested in or concerned with legislation on drugs.

Two new laws were passed by Congress in its ninety-first session and were signed by the President in 1970. The new laws are commonly known as the Comprehensive Drug Abuse Prevention and Control Act and the Drug Abuse Education Act. These laws need to be studied in detail for full understandings of their content, but the parts (summarized by the team of experts) that pertain to heroin are in turn condensed below.

The Federal penalty for unlawful manufacture, distribution, dispensation, or possession with the intent to manufacture, distribute, or dispense narcotics (heroin, opium, morphine, cocaine) on conviction is as follows:

First offense	Not more than 15 years in prison, fine of $25,000 (either or both).
Second and subsequent offenses	Not more than 30 years in prison, fine of not more than $50,000 (either or both).

If imprisoned, the heroin offender cannot be considered for parole for three years if he has no prior conviction, or for six years if there has been a prior conviction.

Simple possession of a controlled drug that has been illegally obtained (heroin cannot be legally obtained in the United States) calls for imprisonment for one year or less, a fine of $5,000 or less, or both these penalties. For second or third convictions imprisonment **can** be increased up to two years and the fine up to $10,000 or both of these penalties. However, the court may substitute probation up to one year and if the probation is not violated charges may be dismissed and the person discharged. If the offender is under 21 years of age and charges are dismissed, he may apply to have **all** records removed.

Other penalties are complex and must be studied in the original, the four experts suggest. Continuing criminal activity in the breaking of drug laws, for example, may result in life imprisonment.

2

some biological considerations

Heroin has both subjective and physiological effects on humans, some of which can be predicted with reasonable certainty. Chemical studies of the structures of morphine and heroin have resulted in identification of certain biological effects of these drugs that are now well known to physicians. Chemical changes induced by enzymes in the body, however, may lead to unpredictable results in terms of accelerated or diminished biological activities for any particular person or addict. Thus, in general the metabolism of the opiates, including morphine and heroin, is well known to physicians, so far as the findings of research reveal today.

Addicts themselves tend to know the effects, without the knowledge of the metabolic processes by which they are produced. There is still a vast amount of knowledge to be learned about heroin and the way in which it is handled in the body.

how the body handles morphine
and heroin

Way, E. Leong and T. K. Adler. "The Biological Disposition of Morphine and its Surrogates—4," WHO Bulletin, 27: 359-394, 1962.

Two pharmacologists of the University of California Medical Center in San Francisco discuss the biological disposition of heroin in the body as a part of a much broader exposition of what happens to morphine.

Capable chemists can, in many instances, predict from the chemical structure of a compound how the body will react to it. What they are often unable to predict is how the body may change the chemical structure of a substance through enzyme actions that may enhance the activities of the drug or may diminish its effects. In other words, effects do not depend solely on the chemical structure of a substance.

The use of various dyes to stain certain drugs, the use of tracer techniques to follow the disposition of compound parts labelled with radioactive substances, separation of the studied materials from body tissues and fluids and other techniques have permitted the scientists to learn much about what happens to drugs in the body.

It has been found that heroin in the brain and body tissues rapidly decreases because it is changed to morphine and monoacetylmorphine. Excretion from the body is not very important. Biotransformation (change of the drug into another chemical compound by biological means) is the principal limiting factor. Very little morphine and its derivatives or substitutes such as heroin is found in the brain. There is some excretion of the substance, however, in the feces, urine, bile, saliva, tears, sweat and milk, even though the amounts disposed of are in trace amounts only. The metabolic products of heroin in the body are mostly bound morphine, some free morphine, and a trace of 6-acetylmorphine. The discovery that codeine, too, is chemically changed in part to morphine in the body is information that has been gained only recently.

Enzymes and the liver are important in bringing about a union of morphine with some other substance. This conjugation or combining process appears to be a major way in which morphine and its related compounds, such as heroin, are disposed of by biological processes. The union of morphine, for example, with gluronic acid produces morphine monoglucuronide, which is less active than the original morphine.

Complete metabolic disposition of morphine and heroin is not known. Union with other tissues, alteration of chemical structure, the splitting of compounds by the addition of water are probably the principal metabolic pathways, but oxidation may be involved and it is likely that various metabolic pathways in the body are involved in the disposition of morphine and heroin.

heroin and the brain

Way, E. Leong. "Accessibility of Morphine to the Brain and its Pharmacologic Implications," Journal of Formosa Medical Association, 62: 490–497, June 28, 1963.

A physiologist of the University of Hong Kong and the Department of Pharmacology of the University of California Medical Center says that it is generally recognized that heroin has more pronounced effects and greater liability of addiction than morphine, but in the body heroin is rapidly and almost completely changed to morphine.

The Hong Kong scientist studied this apparent discrepancy with special attention to the uptake and metabolism of heroin by the brain. With mice, he found that within 2½ minutes heroin would be split by enzymes of the liver, kidney, blood and brain, in that order of activity, into morphine.

The uptake of heroin by the brain was found to be extremely rapid in mice, with only 30 seconds needed after injection, but within 5 minutes heroin could no longer be detected, but morphine levels were high and could be detected even after 30 minutes. In other words, heroin is rapidly absorbed and rapidly converted to monoacetylmorphine first and then into morphine. Of these three compounds, heroin was found to be the most toxic, then monoacetyl morphine and morphine the least toxic, when injected by vein.

However, when the three drugs were injected directly into brain tissue (rather than into a blood vessel) morphine was found to be about 3 times as toxic as heroin and 6 times as toxic as monoacetyl morphine. When heroin is broken down in the body outside of the central nervous system the new compounds have a difficult time entering nerve tissue, so the process is, in effect, one of detoxification. However, if the breakdown of heroin occurs in the brain the liberation of the more toxic morphine at that point would result in more toxic effects.

effects of the opiates

Vandam, Leroy D. "Clinical Pharmacology of the Narcotic Analgesics," Clinical Pharmacology and Therapeutics, 3: 827-838, November–December 1962.

A doctor from Peter Bent Brigham Hospital and Harvard Medical School observes that opium has been used for the relief of pain as far back as records go. Although morphine is the most widely used pain killer today this narcotic has undesirable effects that prompt a continuing search for something better.

The relief of pain without disturbance of other sensations may be the only valid reason for using a narcotic pain killer, says Doctor Vandam. Just how a narcotic acts in the central nervous system has never been clarified. Depending on the dosage the effects of most narcotics last from two to four hours so far as the elimination or reduction of pain is concerned, but other physiological reactions occur for many hours more.

Sedation and mood alterations may or may not be advantageous. Feelings of well-being, apprehension, drowsiness, lethargy, apathy and mental confusion have been reported by various persons. Occasionally morphine leads to agitation and excitement, particularly in women. In many patients the changes caused by the narcotic can be attributed to the personality of the subject.

Respiratory effects occur after all of the narcotics. Depression of breathing occurs and research has shown that the respiratory center of the brain becomes less sensitive to the stimulus of carbon dioxide or the hydrogen ion. Elderly people appear to be particularly susceptible to respiratory depression from narcotics. The giving of a narcotic antagonist may lead to a rapid and dramatic recovery from respiratory depression.

Circulatory depression occurs, but is hardly noticeable under ordinary circumstances. Arterial blood pressure declines and the pulse may slow to some extent. The older person is especially apt to develop low blood pressure after narcotics.

Nausea and vomiting may be of utmost concern to the patient, but are of little importance compared to the significance of respiratory and circulatory effects, from a medical viewpoint.

Tolerance, addiction and habituation occur with all of the narcotic drugs. Tolerance (diminishing effect of the same dosage) is produced by some little-understood process. Habituation reflects an emotional or psychological dependence on a drug. Addiction has occurred when a person develops a physical dependence for a drug, so that withdrawal symptoms occur if the person does not have his drug on schedule. [Psychological dependence is also a major part of addiction.—Ed.] The addiction potential of heroin is especially high and accounts for its prohibition by law.

effects of heroin and morphine
on non-addicts

Smith, Gene M. and Henry K. Beecher. "Subjective Effects of Heroin and Morphine in Normal Subjects," Journal of Pharmacology and Experimental Therapy, 136: 47–52, April 1962.

Two members of the Harvard Medical School report a study of the effects of heroin, morphine, and a placebo on 24 healthy college men who were not addicted to drugs. Effects of heroin on non-addicts have seldom been studied.

A checklist of 90 items measured reactions of the subjects at one-half hour, two hours, three hours and four hours after they were given injections under the skin. At least one week separated the three injections given each subject.

The principal physical reactions to both heroin and morphine involved dizziness, itching, blurring of vision, numbness and nausea.

The subjects reported mental clouding more often from heroin than from morphine, although with either they felt "fuzzy-headed," mentally slow, groggy, dreamy and mentally cloudy.

Both heroin and morphine produced feelings of dejection, unfriendliness, anxiety and insecurity and significant reduction of physical activities.

Although the effects of heroin and morphine were quite similar, three significant differences between these two drugs were found: 1) the effects of heroin were stronger; 2) effects reached a peak sooner with heroin, and 3) there was greater improvement in mood between the first and following periods of testing on "heroin" days than on "morphine" days. The investigators had no explanation for the latter finding.

Heroin produced more unpleasant side effects than morphine, especially in regard to excessive sweating and inability to focus the eyes. Both opiates, however, produced unpleasant side effects. Even with a dosage of 4 milligrams of heroin to 10 milligrams of morphine the side effects of heroin were more severe and more unpleasant.

study of sleep patterns suggests that heroin disturbs normal brain function

Lewis, S. A., I. Oswald, J. I. Evans, M. O. Akindele and S. L. Tompsett. "Heroin and Human Sleep," Electroencephalography and Clinical Neurophysiology, 28: 374–381, April 1970.

Five English scientists observe that there has been little research on the effects of narcotics such as morphine or heroin on sleep.

At least one study has shown that narcotics reduce the amount of rapid eye movements (REM) during sleep. The rapid eye movement delay in returning to normal during a two-months withdrawal period from amphetamines that was observed in one study has suggested that there may be abnormalities of brain function that continue for some time after a drug has been withdrawn.

This team of British investigators studied the matter in four male subjects. It was found that the injection of heroin under the skin immediately decreased the proportion of rapid eye movements during sleep, with a gradual restoration to near normal (but incomplete return) within three days of administration of heroin. On withdrawal there was an immediate rise in the proportion of eye movements during sleep. This rebound phenomenon that followed heroin withdrawal was still being sustained two and three months afterwards in two of the subjects.

The authors observe that heroin is often thought of as an effective hypnotic when sleep is disturbed by pain, but they believe heroin acts instead to disturb sleep from its normal pattern. Whatever the explanation, there appears to be a prolonged physiological recovery, so far as sleep is concerned, after the taking of heroin. In short, the researchers contend that heroin can cause abnormalities of brain function that persist for weeks or months after withdrawal of the drug, although the exact nature of these abnormalities is unknown.

mental efficiency reduced by heroin
or morphine

Smith, Gene M., Charles W. Semke and Henry K. Beecher. "Objective Evidence of Mental Effects of Heroin, Morphine and Placebo in Normal Subjects," Journal of Pharmacology and Experimental Therapy, 136: 53–58, April 1962.

Three members of the Harvard Medical School observe that since most persons who are not addicted to opiates report being mentally clouded after receiving narcotics it should be expected that opiates would impair performance on objective tests of perception, memory, learning and reasoning. However, this possibility had been studied little, with inconclusive results.

In this investigation 48 college males who were not addicted to narcotics were tested for mental performance after injections of heroin, morphine, and a placebo separately.

It was found that heroin and morphine both caused significant impairment of mental performance, with definite evidence of mental impairment. The reduction of mental efficiency was primarily one of speed. Mental functioning was damaged earlier and to a greater extent by heroin than by morphine, even though the amount of morphine given was 2½ times greater than the amount of heroin injected.

Significant mental impairment was shown as early as 40 minutes and as late as five hours and 40 minutes after administration of morphine.

reduction of physical activity by heroin

Fraser, H. F., B. E. Jones, D. E. Rosenberg and A. K. Thompson. "Effects of Addiction to Intravenous Heroin on Patterns of Physical Activity in Man," Clinical Pharmacology and Therapeutics, 4: 188–196, March–April 1963.

A group of doctors from Lexington, Kentucky with the National Institute of Mental Health, Addiction Research Center, report the results of a study of physical activity in five prisoner addicts who went without the drug but were given placebos for 30 days of observations and were then given heroin by injection for 60 days. The amount of physical movement of the addicts was measured with a pedometer. Hours lying down, sleeping, and time away from the research ward were recorded also.

At first heroin increased physical activity, but after three or four days activities became depressed. As the patients continued to receive heroin they retreated from all forms of physical activity and social contacts and spent more time lying on their beds with eyes closed and listening to music in a sedated state. The study revealed a reduced ability to respond to stimuli in the environment.

Comments of the subjects participating in the heroin study included remarks such as the following:

"When drugs are in me, I'm content to do less . . . so I keep to myself."

"When I'm on dope I can sleep in the daytime as well as at night . . . and time goes faster."

"The drug made me sleepy and people irritated me, so I go to my room."

"For the first time . . . I could sit down, lie down, or stand for 20 minutes without doing something different . . . on that drug I wanted to be by myself . . ."

"I didn't want to be bothered with other people."

3

addiction as an occupational hazard

In medicine, nursing, dentistry and certain paramedical sciences where access to drugs may exist, there is always the potential that a person may begin to abuse drugs. Nearly 15 years ago the rate of addiction among physicians was reputed to be 30 times that of the layman, and hospital admissions for drug abuse eight times as great. Although modern control efforts involving better and earlier alerting of medical students to the hazards and legal consequences of drug abuse have been reported as lowering addiction rates among professional persons in medicine and associated paramedical sciences, addiction to drugs is still considered among the well-informed as an occupational hazard of the field of medicine.

the physician who turned to drugs

"Speed Can Trap the Doctor, Too," Hospital Physician, 6: 65–67, 124 (No. 10), October 1970.

A physician, identified by the letter X, tells of his problems and degradation that began with amphetamine abuse.

Physicians have a higher rate of drug dependence than that of the general population, despite warnings of their special vulnerability to addiction. The vast majority of doctors resist the temptation to use drugs for an escape from fatigue, anxiety, or boredom. Doctor X comments: ". . . my colleagues . . . must have known that I was doing something to my brain. They'd have done me a great favor if they had spoken to me about it or taken some official action . . ."

Dr. X says that for a couple of years he had taken amphetamines occasionally as a mood elevator after a rough day, a series of night calls, or after distress of a patient for whom he was responsible. He had taken amphetamines during medical school to get through final examinations, and in medical practice he soon found himself resorting to amphetamines again after fatigue, restlessness, and hostility involving his wife's family, as well as having a feeling that perhaps he was in the wrong occupation and should not have been a physician.

Through the use of stimulants he was able to read, write, and paint in addition to his medical practice, although he would be well fatigued the next day. He would dispel the fatigue with amphetamines. Then, he found that the stimulants led him away from his wife to women and promiscuity.

Dr. X found that amphetamines made him extremely talkative and impaired his judgment. Often his words were not appropriate to the situation. Physical hyperactivity occurred, along with abrupt, poorly coordinated movements. He found himself knocking over his coffee cup after or before surgery. The loss of control soon extended to handwriting. He found himself becoming irritable and impatient with both friends and patients. Then, impairment of speech and memory followed. The loss of memory was mostly for recent events. Deep fissures began to appear in the cuticle of the fingers, the pupils of his eyes began to enlarge, and tensions of the facial muscles began to distort his normal expression. All of these changes were subtle and perhaps hard to detect.

The deterioration of judgment, morals, and personality were most pronounced, according to Dr. X. His patients began to leave him. One patient told him she was changing to another physician because he was no longer patient, that he had changed, that he had lost the "homey" personal way that she had liked. Other patients just stopped coming. In a period of four months he lost one-third of his total practice. He felt great remorse for his debaucheries, his faithlessness to his family, the deterioration of his health and ideals and the decline of his practice and bank account. Next, he was blackmailed for impairing the morals of a minor, and had a mental crackup, was confined to a psychiatric hospital, and divorced by his wife. After two years of treatment he is now trying to practice medicine again without drugs.

[While the facts are not questioned, the reader is cautioned that this is a single anecdotal record.—Ed.]

addict nurses

Poplar, Jimmie F. "Characteristics of Nurse Addicts," American Journal of Nursing, 69: 117–119, January 1969.

A graduate nurse and Clinical Research Center specialist at Lexington, Kentucky reports on her observations of 90 registered nurses who were receiving treatment for narcotic addiction in the latter facility.

Many of the nurses feared that they would lose their licenses, showed considerable guilt, and often exhibited signs of panic. The nurses were worried about three things in particular after their impending discharges from treatment: 1) Should they tell any new employers of their addiction experience? 2) Should they handle keys to narcotics supplies? 3) Who could they turn to in time of need? Most of the nurses wanted someone to know about their problem and most felt that they would feel more secure if they did not have access to the keys to narcotics.

The nursing group was found to be distinctly different from the average woman addict, both through observations on the part of the hospital staff and from the results of psychological tests. First, the nurses became addicted as adults, not as adolescents, and began using drugs to relieve pain or for escape from stresses rather than for "kicks." Their drug use was a solitary experience rather than in the company of others. When the cost of drugs became too expensive the nurses did not resort to prostitution, shoplifting, or other measures, but used theft in the working situation, prescriptions by physicians, or forged prescriptions to obtain their drugs.

The nurses looked upon themselves as being mentally ill and believed that they should be forced to accept psychiatric care. Most volunteered for treatment.

Most of the nurse-addicts came from stable and intact homes and most of them had close relationships with their families. There was no background of childhood or adolescent problems severe enough to bring them to the attention of the law. Finally, they were more intelligent and better educated than the average woman addict.

The major conclusion about nurse-addicts seems to be that they resort to drugs because of pressures and problems they cannot handle and that after rehabilitation they feel more comfortable if they work in situations where narcotics are not needed by the patients.

drug abuse as an occupational hazard

Middleton, John. "Drug Abuse: Growing Occupational Hazard for Doctors," Hospital Physician, 6: 61-63, 123-124 (No. 10), October 1970.

A survey in 1970 of nearly 1,000 hospital physicians shows that most of them think the use of drugs by medical students has increased about 68 per cent in the past two years. The group also thought there had been an increase of about 39 per cent in the use of drugs by hospital physicians. [The drugs used are not specified.—Ed.]

One correspondent said: "A lot of doctors, like some of today's youth, are kind of loose in their attitude toward drugs . . . . This is a disturbing trend, because I believe drug use can lead to professional death.''

Another correspondent from a hospital where treatment is given to drug addicts observed that physician-addicts are generally multiple drug users. Another reaction was this: "There is definite evidence that the physician who has become dependent on alcohol has a high risk of becoming a drug addict."

This tendency to move on to more dangerous drugs is reflected by the high incidence of narcotic addiction among physicians, now estimated at being from 30 to 100 times that of the general population. "It's nothing short of an occupational hazard," said one psychiatrist.

Stress, fatigue, depression, boredom, self-treatment for illnesses, poor medical education about drugs and the availability of drugs are all contributing factors to physician addiction.

The pattern of drug addiction by physicians is that a doctor starts with heavy use of alcohol to relax after long hours of work, then becomes fearful his excessive drinking may be noticed; so he starts on barbiturates at night and amphetamines during the day. Soon gross errors of judgment, careless mistakes, and indifference expose his use of drugs. One medical addict arrived on a house call, took off his coat, gave himself a shot of meperidine in the presence of the patient and his family, and then said: "Well, now, I've solved my problem. What's yours?" A surgeon cut into a wrong body part, but with no sense of remorse made no serious attempt to repair the damage and remarked he "must have been a little heavy with the knife."

In California it has been found that the physician has the best chance of becoming rehabilitated if he is permitted to continue practicing medicine under restraints. His narcotic license is removed, other physicians watch him, and he is warned that his license will be revoked unless he gives up drugs. These doctors under discipline must report regularly to the Board of Medical Examiners for five years. If there is a second offense, 85 per cent of the violators have their licenses revoked or suspended immediately. If the physician then seeks professional treatment he has a chance to get his license back ultimately. Recovery occurs in 85 per cent of the doctor-addicts under this kind of discipline.

physicians and drugs

Vaillant, George E., Jane R. Brighton, and Charles McArthur. "Physicians' Use of Mood-Altering Drugs," New England Journal of Medicine, 282: 365–370 (No. 7), February 12, 1970.

A physician and two associates of Tufts University School of Medicine and the Harvard University Health Services observe that in recent years evidence has been forthcoming that the abuse of alcohol and mood-altering drugs may be the most common sign of psychiatric illness in physicians.

Among doctors admitted for psychiatric reasons to the Mayo Clinic it was found that 50 per cent showed dependence on alcohol or drugs, and that 23 per cent were dependent on both. Three other studies of physicians hospitalized for mental illness found that approximately 50 per cent were addicted to alcohol or drugs.

There is other evidence that physicians in general (those who do not seek psychiatric help) abuse drugs more than the population at large. In California, from one to two per cent have been found to be drug abusers. Over a period of 25 years about one-half of one per cent of licensed physicians in the state of New York were reported as narcotic addicts. In contrast, only about 1 in 1,000 American males in the age group 20 to 50 years becomes addicted to narcotics and most of these addicts come from the slums. [However, it can be noted that most physicians never abuse drugs.—Ed.]

In this study 258 men who were chosen for the investigation were followed to their death or to the present in respect to their use of drugs, alcohol or tobacco. All were college sophomores and to be accepted into the study each subject had to be considered by the college health service, the dean's office, and dormitory staff members as comparatively free of physical, emotional, and academic problems. Of the original group 46 eventually became physicians, only one of whom has died. About every two years all of the men were followed by extensive questionnaires and some personal interviews. After 30 years there has been no evidence that false information has been given.

It was found that physicians drank no more alcohol and smoked no more cigarettes than their fellow normal subjects in the study. However, in respect to drug abuse, the physicians were found to use amphetamines and tranquilizers regularly twice as often as the other persons in the study, and to use sedatives about three times as often as the other non-physicians.

Medicine is hard work for anyone and physicians who are narcotic addicts give "overwork" as the most common explanation of why they take narcotics, but psychiatric study of doctors suggests that the availability of drugs and hard work may not be a sufficient explanation. Psychiatric reasons may be more important. Depression may be a significant symptom.

Medical schools must assume a more important role in orienting their students that they represent a high-risk population for drug abuse and that no physician should ever write himself a self-prescription for drugs.

what happens to doctors who turn to drugs?

Putnam, Peter L. and Everett H. Ellinwood, Jr. "Narcotic Addiction Among Physicians: A Ten-Year Follow-up," American Journal of Psychiatry, 122: 745–748, January 1966.

Two physicians of the National Institute of Mental Health and Duke University Medical Center respectively observe that little is known about what happens to physicians who become drug addicts.

In this study the doctors compared the experiences of 68 doctor addicts who were discharged from the U.S. Public Health Service Hospital in Lexington after treatment, with 68 other physicians used as a control group.

Chronic fatigue and physical illness were the primary reasons given by the addict doctors for the self-administration of narcotics, although multiple other factors were also involved, such as availability of a drug.

Ten years after discharge from the Lexington Hospital only 57 per cent of the physicians were still listed in the American Medical Association directories of members, as compared to 81 per cent of the control, non-addict group. The doctors who had used drugs moved from city to city twice as often as the other physicians. Previous research has shown that the death rate of addict-physicians is high (due to physical illness), that the suicide rate amounts to about eight or nine per cent and that repeated hospitalization and finally imprisonment occurs. Loss of medical license and hospital expenses often create economic problems for the physicians who have become addicts.

4

the heroin addict

What kind of person is the heroin addict? Do the seeds of his destruction lie within his own personality or should the fault of his deterioration be shifted to his family and to society?

In general, heroin addicts have a high representation in terms of general maladjustment, parental neglect, quarrels among parents, and delinquency. Often heroin addiction appears to be in part a sociological problem, but also a personal problem that reflects the problems of an inadequate personality. The family background may be faulty also, regardless of the social status and prominence of the latter, but the problems of the addict may stem not from his family, but from his own personal deficiencies and peer group associations.

Heroin addicts tend to form their own exclusive groups and to show behavior characteristics that are different from normal populations or abusers of other substances, such as alcohol. Heroin addicts are apt to be more non-conforming and to reject the objectives in life that others in the community find acceptable. Generally there is a history of deviant behavior even before the taking of drugs begins. Study of the wives of drug addicts suggests that the latter are "weak men" and that the women who marry addicts and remain married to them have personalities that obligate them to remain involved with weak men.

Whatever the basic roots of individual addiction may be, there is evidence that the first use of heroin takes place under varying circumstances that may involve peer group pressure, ignorance, feelings of low self-esteem and depression, pain, or other conditions from which an escape is sought.

Although in the past some persons have opposed drug abuse education in the conviction that it would merely create more addicts, the modern viewpoint is that both social controls and education are needed in efforts to reduce and prevent heroin addiction in our society.

the easy rider syndrome in drug addicts

Wellisch, David K., George R. Gay and Roseann McEntee. "The Easy Rider Syndrome: A Pattern of Hetero- and Homosexual Relationships in a Heroin Addict Population," Family Process, 9: 425–430 (No. 4), December 1970.

A psychologist, a physician, and a nurse of the Drug Detoxification Section of the Haight-Ashbury Medical Clinic in San Francisco report on their experiences in the treatment of nearly 1,000 cases of heroin withdrawal in approximately one year of time. The team of investigators interviewed as many as 60 patients in an afternoon.

The three professionals came to recognize an inter-personal relationship over and over again in the treated heroin users. This relationship was named the "Easy Rider Syndrome" because in addict couples, regardless as to whether they were married, unmarried, or homosexuals, one partner was supported or taken care of by the other, so became an "easy rider" throughout the relationship and appeared to be involved in such a relationship to life in general. This style of life appeared to evolve after at least one year of heavy heroin usage.

Psychological testing of the partners in the "Easy Rider Syndrome" revealed high psychopathic, mania, and depression scores. Females typically had fathers who were inept, alcoholic, or both and who had often beaten the daughter and sexually abused her. The female partners adopted a pseudo-mother role and frequently prostituted herself to keep the heroin coming in daily.

When the symptoms of heroin withdrawal are resolved an

enormous boredom factor must be resolved also, the research team found, because the activities of the couple no longer center around heroin. This factor was especially true for the female, whose total daily life consisted of prostituting herself, buying heroin, and bringing it home to "easy rider." The male, used to sitting or lying around the house "stoned" on heroin a good deal of the time, may now find himself highly anxious and agitated. Separation or divorce may follow, since the main bonds prior to "kicking" the heroin habit were based on use of the drug. The couple often cannot face the many problems that were hidden with heroin. The problems that led to heroin use in the first place are still present and cannot be ignored, or the "easy rider" and his girl will be pushed back into the heroin lifestyle that is familiar to them.

why young people turn to drugs

Carson, Doyle I. and Jerry M. Lewis. "Factors Influencing Drug Abuse in Young People," Texas Medicine, 66: 50–57 (No. 1), January 1970.

Two physicians of the Timberlawn Foundation in Dallas, Texas express their convictions that drug abuse in young people should be considered from three different viewpoints: 1) the influences of cultural factors; 2) the influences of disturbed, pathological families, and 3) the psychological problems of the young individual abuser of drugs.

The physicians observe that cultures change and in America the old virtues of thrift and chastity in a work-oriented society have now been replaced in a culture of material abundance with the new message of "do it now." The past seems distant, the future improbable, and the here and now infinitely more important to the young person. When drugs are frequently used in our present culture to alleviate feelings of anxiety, worry, stress or psychological pain, there is less motivation to find other solutions to life problems. The young people have spent a major portion of their lives in a culture that is different than it was a few decades ago. Although the physicians are concerned about the potentially destructive impact of a drug-centered life for young people, they see the problem as part of a gradually evolving "chemical culture."

Each family evolves a "system" for being a family. In some cases there is warmth and open expression of affection in which cases people are able to talk, hug, and kiss freely. In another family the direct expression of affection may be forbidden. Family systems are being studied currently in many dimensions, such as those of family decision making, conflict resolution, communication patterns, myth formations and so on. Some research demonstrates the impact of grossly disturbed families on the adolescent, so that relationships to drug abuse may be found. More study is needed of the impact of family systems on the use of drugs in young people.

A bewildering complexity of psychological factors seems to be involved in the dependence on drugs by adolescents. The two Dallas physicians have found in their clinical work that drug-dependent adolescents are seriously disturbed and suggest that they should be differentiated from young people who use drugs out of curiosity but do not become dependent on them. Some of the more common psychological problems that are associated with the use of drugs in young people are as follows: 1) under-achievement in school and work situations; 2) loneliness of unhappy, isolated adolescents who seem to lack the capacity for warm, human relationships; 3) mistrust and fear of closeness, especially of adults (amphetamines especially increase mistrust and paranoid illness); 4) identity of self with a way of living, a philosophy, a code of values which may represent difficulty in developing an acceptable self; 5) sexual conflicts; 6) a struggle between feelings of dependency and independence; 7) rebellion; 8) feelings of aggression, and 9) tendencies toward self-destruction; for some the use of drugs is a slow suicide.

reasons for drugs

Ponting, L. I. and C. S. Nicol. "Drug dependence among patients attending a Department of Venereology," British Journal of Venereal Disease, 46: 111–113, April 1970.

An English physician and an associate at a Venereal Disease Clinic in London interviewed 206 patients who were receiving treatment for venereal disease, but who also admitted the use of drugs.

Among information obtained by the interviewers were 15 expressed reasons why the patients had turned to drugs, as follows:

1. A need for keeping awake at work or at parties.
2. Just for kicks.
3. Because it was the thing being done.

4. Curiosity.
5. Boredom.
6. An inability to make friends.
7. Because of an introverted personality.
8. Depression.
9. Because of an inferiority complex.
10. For escape from reality.
11. Because of loneliness.
12. Because of searching for something and never finding it.
13. For relaxation.
14. Because of the belief perception would be increased.
15. Because hemp was not considered a drug in the areas from which certain patients came.

Of the 206 drug users 15 males and nine females had had previous psychiatric care (not necessarily for drug usage). Nineteen males and eight females (including four prostitutes) had been in trouble with the police (but not necessarily for drug taking).

The majority had been introduced to drugs by friends. At the time of the study nine admitted they were now dependent on drugs, 44 said they used drugs regularly, 130 affirmed they used drugs occasionally and 23 said they had taken drugs only once.

It is difficult to judge whether the expressed reasons for the use of drugs were the genuine ones, but they were reasons the users believed to be genuine or else reasons they were willing to admit, real or not.

factors involved in the first use of heroin

Bowden, Charles L. "Determinants of Initial Use of Opioids,"
Comprehensive Psychiatry, 12: 136–140, March 1971.

A member of the University of Texas Medical School at San
Antonio reports a study based upon his experiences with addicts at the Clinical Research Center in Lexington, Kentucky
regarding factors involved in a first use of heroin.

The physician found eight different categories of factors
associated with the beginning use of heroin, as follows: 1) a
condition of low-self esteem and depression; 2) efforts to
solve problems of social isolation or sexual inadequacy;
3) persuasion by a heroin addict; 4) ignorance of the effects
of the opiate drugs; 5) pleasure-seeking by young persons
with serious emotional disturbances; 6) to achieve relief from
anxiety and unpleasant feelings; 7) to achieve relief from
pain, and 8) miscellaneous other factors, such as curiosity,
use of other drugs, a symbolic striking out against parents,
society or others or to curb anger and pugnacious behavior.

Case studies included an 18-year old boy who refused the
efforts of friends to get him to use heroin for four years, but
who gave in to their urgings when he was put out of his home
by his mother who wanted to make a man of him. It was
Christmas eve, he was despondent, had a low opinion of himself and accidentally encountered an addict acquaintance who
talked him into trying heroin.

In another instance a 20-year old male tried heroin when
a friend accused him of being a coward and was able to
supply the heroin for an injection.

A 17-year old boy had been drinking a pint of whiskey daily and at parties he would get drunk, argumentative and into fights. When he saw how heroin calmed a friend he did not hesitate to use it, partly because he was ignorant of its addictive qualities and because he became calm when he used the drug.

A 40-year old man had painful hemorrhoids and an intolerance to pain. Two heroin addicts in his apartment said they had something to stop his pain. After using heroin for a week he "didn't have no choice."

The Texas doctor believes that the availability of heroin should be curtailed, and that educational programs should be more widespread. Education efforts should be made before the age of risk and should be most intensive in areas of high risk, and should be part of a broader health education program.

seven kinds of drug addicts

Pinney, Jr., Edward L. *"Determinants for the Classification of Drug Addicts," Diseases of the Nervous System, 27: 55-59, January 1966.*

A physician of the Cumberland Medical Center in Brooklyn reports that from his experiences with drug addicts he has concluded that social, psychiatric, and economic factors, as well as accidents of birth, give rise to different kinds of addicts. In his judgment there are seven different categories of narcotic addiction, as follows.

1 *The mendicant addict* begs to be given drugs free and he attends clinics; he may sometimes be maintained safely on other drugs than the one to which he is primarily addicted.

2 *The affluent addict* takes drugs for pleasure and excitement. He is economically secure and does not usually come for treatment. Psychiatric illness may occur in this group of addicts, but only in a minority.

3 *The socially deficient addict* is one who uses drugs in an attempt to remedy some social defect. He wants to belong to some gang or group. Social or environmental conditions are important factors in his addiction. Addicts of this group have severe personality disorders and a moderate number are psychotic and schizophrenic.

4 *The defiant (dyssocial) addict* takes drugs as part of his "cool" defiance. He talks with bravado. Some members of this group have low intelligence and may be quite deteriorated. They may be petty criminals. Sometimes they give up drugs as they get older.

5 *Iatrogenic addicts* have become addicted to drugs during medical treatment. Patients who have a fatal illness and suffer pain may be maintained with narcotics until death as a humanitarian measure.

6 *The addict with psychosis* is deteriorated in personality, often taken advantage of by other addicts, may commit major crimes and needs treatment for his basic mental illness after removal from a drug.

7 *The congenital addict* is the newborn baby who is addicted to a drug because the mother was taking a narcotic during pregnancy. Under proper hospital and medical treatment this kind of addict can be withdrawn from drugs safely. The final outcome will probably be determined by the future environment, according to Doctor Pinney. [Some authorities would insist that the newborn could be dependent upon drugs, but that use of the term "addicted" to describe an infant is not the term to be preferred.—Ed.]

the adolescent heroin addict

Boyd, Philip. "Heroin Addiction in Adolescents," Journal of Psychosomatic Research, 14: 295–301, September 1970.

A faculty member of the Middlesex Hospital Medical School in London reports that in England the problem of addiction has risen seven fold from 1961 to 1970.

In discussing the problem of heroin addiction Doctor Boyd observes that the personality structure of many young people is abnormally fragile and that they may be easily confused by changes in personal, social and moral values of an affluent and permissive society.

Doctor Boyd says that the emotionally normal and mature person infrequently becomes addicted to heroin. The same is true for the adolescent who is making sound progress toward the development of his own maturity.

The adolescent who turns to drugs profoundly changes his chance of normal development. At this point Doctor Boyd says the adolescent is in need of psychiatric care.

Sometimes an adolescent will claim to be a narcotic addict when he is not. Experience at the English clinics indicates that his purpose is to obtain drugs with which he can experiment, make money by sale of the drug on the black market, or to get the drug for someone else.

The adolescent drug abuser is apt to be lonely and without a trustworthy friend. He is apt to have an intense underlying suspicion of others, and especially of adults in authority. Friendships seldom last long. The addict is almost always chronically depressed and poorly integrated in a sexual way. His reaction to an adult woman may appear to be passive and submissive, but may suddenly explode to hostility and destructiveness with massive verbal obscenities.

The young user of heroin will generally have a sense of guilt and be well aware of his emptiness and failure.

The basic problem of heroin addiction in the adolescent is one of a severe emotional and personality disturbance at a critical period of development, says Dr. Boyd. The outlook is poor, but young people need to learn to deal with drugs as a hazard of growing up in this modern world.

the stand up cat

Feldman, Harvey W. "Ideological Supports to Becoming and Remaining a Heroin Addict," Journal of Health and Social Behavior, 9: 131–139, June 1968.

A faculty member of Brandeis University questions the almost universal conclusion that drug users in a slum community have become addicted because they are maladjusted, immature, hostile, and generally weak in personality.

The author advances the concept of the "stand up cat" as a person in the neighborhood and slum who is responsible for the spread of heroin usage. The stand up cat has a reputation for roughness, daring, and an ability to face dangerous situations that gives him a leadership position in the slums. Those younger or less able adolescents who strive for recognition and identification are apt to emulate the stand up cat. By doing so these lesser members of the social network of the slums hope to achieve a high status and prestige.

Experimentation with drugs on the part of the stand up cat reflects his willingness to engage in another activity possessed of danger and rebellion against authority. Followers who are striving to achieve the status of the stand up cat may embark upon the use of heroin on an epidemic scale. It is not an attempt to resolve an inner emotional problem, nor a defeatist reaction to the slums, but an effort to enhance his status and prestige that causes the young slum dweller to begin taking heroin.

As Professor Feldman expresses it, movement into the use of heroin becomes a route to becoming a somebody in the lifestyle of the admired stand up cat.

family backgrounds of the heroin addict

Torda, Clara. "Comments on the Character Structure and Psychodynamic Processes of Heroin Addicts," Perceptual and Motor Skills, 27: 143–146, August 1968.

A faculty member of the Downstate Medical College of the State University of New York reports the results of a study of differences of family backgrounds of 30 heroin addicts as compared to 30 non-users of drugs.

The heroin addicts were more likely to come from families in which the mother was dominant, the father weak and possibly alcoholic as well as disinterested in his family. The father was apt to have been absent from the family during early years of the heroin addict. The mother was apt to have had no genuine love of the child.

The infant-raising practices of the mother were apt to be of such a nature that any independent activity, self-expression, or self-assertion on the part of the child was apt to be punished, so that the child was left with a feeling of helplessness and worthlessness, followed in turn by frustration, hypersensitivity and other problems.

To the developing heroin addict his childhood became a source of perpetual frustration, hostility, self-hatred, hopelessness, lack of trust in other people, and daydreaming evasion of his problems. His idealized self-image was apt to become that of a quiet, untroubled, and contemplative man, according to Professor Torda, so that in heroin he began to find "all his needs being fulfilled."

Thus, from the study of 30 cases one might suggest that the heroin addict appears to be a loner who has never known genuine love or happiness and who turns to heroin as a welcome, though temporary, relief from his internal problems.

the drug addict

Remmen, E. T. "The Treatment of Narcotic Addiction," Western Medicine, 3: 165, May 1962.

A medical editor, in discussing the treatment of the narcotic addict, says it must be remembered that he is not a normal, sound, well-balanced individual.

Doctor Remmen says the drug addict represents a small percentage of the human race and that he is "likely to be rather passive, easily discouraged, dependent and inadequate. He may feel unwanted, unloved, and unsuccessful. He may have been rejected by one or both parents. If he is a member of a minority race, this may add to his sense of frustration and rejection."

The physician observes that many serious mental illnesses can be found among narcotic addicts from which they find temporary relief with heroin. Many are seriously immature and have few friends, if any, except among other addicts. Sexual adjustment is poor and the sexual drive is reduced when heroin usage becomes heavy.

In Doctor Remmen's opinion the addiction to drugs results from emotional problems and mental illnesses. Addiction is the result, rather than the cause, of basic problems.

wives of drug addicts

Taylor, Susan D., Mary Wilbur and Robert Osnos. "The Wives of Drug Addicts," American Journal of Psychiatry, 123: 585-591, November 1966.

A nurse, a social worker, and a psychiatrist of New York City combined their efforts in the study of 16 couples where the husbands were undergoing treatment for drug addiction.

A questionnaire and interview study led the investigators to conclude that most of the men had serious character disorders, usually of the passive-aggressive type. In general the wives were stronger and functioned more adequately than the husbands, although in relationships with their own families the former had many unresolved problems, mostly centering around a weak man as a father and antagonism with a mother.

The research team concluded from their study that the wives of drug addicts have personality structures that obligate them to remain involved with weak men whom they can dominate and who make a minimum sexual demand upon them.

use of drugs by young persons

Kyger, Kent. "VI. The Drug Culture," Journal of the Tennessee Medical Association, 64: 1043-1048, December 1971.

A psychiatrist of the Vanderbilt University School of Medicine reflects on the use of drugs by young persons between 13 and 18 years of age. His observations and tentative conclusions are based upon his experience with young users of drugs with whom he has come into contact during his private practice of psychiatry.

Although the Vanderbilt psychiatrist does not specifically mention why young people use heroin, he does express his professional viewpoints and clinical experience as to why they turn to drugs in general. Since most heroin users have tried other drugs his remarks appear pertinent.

Doctor Kyger believes the son of a successful, busy father is a likely candidate for drug abuse, because he has often been neglected in an emotional way, so that there is no relationship of affection on which constructive discipline can be built. Also, such a child usually has the money with which to buy drugs.

Curiosity and the desire to experience new and altered sensations are often the cause of using drugs such as LSD. Marijuana users, on the other hand, are apt to use the drug for its socializing effects. The inebriating effects of marijuana may overcome shyness and inhibitions so that the adolescent who is socially inadequate can often join a group simply by taking drugs. Some adolescents use drugs because they think it is the "in" thing to do.

Some young people use drugs for self treatment of the emotional symptoms they are experiencing, such as depression, insomnia, tension, anxiety, fears, impending psychotic disturbances and so on, according to Doctor Kyger. Others may use drugs in the belief that they can improve the mind for quick learning, or can get "up" for an occasion in lieu of hard work.

Society itself provides a cultural basis for much drug abuse with its boredom, indulgences, modern philosophies and examples of certain "miracle drugs" such as penicillin and other antibiotics from which good has been obtained. Our country consumes more drugs of all kinds than any other nation, says the Vanderbilt psychiatrist. Self-observation, study, and analysis are often replaced with thoughts of "knowing thyself" through the use of drugs that are falsely thought to be "mind revealing."

Emotional development and maturity take time and cannot be hastened by the pressures of society or by turning to drugs, but the pressures and tensions faced by the adolescent today may cause him to think that they can help. Drugs delay treatment, cause emotional regression and provide an escape from reality, and they generally produce an unproductive withdrawal from society, says Dr. Kyger.

5

detection of the heroin addict

Detection of the heroin addict who wishes to conceal his drug abuse is not a simple matter, although medical techniques are improving in this regard. On the basis of symptoms the addict does not usually expose himself if he gets his regular dose of heroin. Under influence of the drug he is comfortable and apparently well-adjusted, but without the drug his personality changes, he may suffer from withdrawal symptoms, and he may become dangerous in his desperate need for his next "fix." Scientific procedures have emerged, however, for the mass screening of large groups of people through analysis of urine, blood studies, and injection of other drugs such as Nalline which bring about observable changes in the heroin addict. Clues to the use of heroin have emerged from studies in which addicts themselves and their families have participated. These clues are suggestive, but not infallible, and must be followed by more definite and objective procedures.

Detection of the addict in a coma because of an overdose of heroin may be especially difficult in some cases. Physicians are beginning to recognize a variety of unusual reactions that may alert them to the possibility of a diagnosis of heroin intoxication.

identification of heroin abusers

Suffolk County Medical Society and District Attorney's Office. "Tips for the Identification of Drug Abusers," New York State Journal of Medicine, 71: 426, February 15, 1971.

A medical and legal group in the state of New York has prepared a tip sheet for the medical identification of drug abusers. A portion of this document is concerned with the identification of heroin, morphine and codeine (opiates) users.

The physical symptoms that may indicate the subject is using heroin include stupor, drowsiness, needle marks on the body, watery eyes, loss of appetite, blood stain on a shirt sleeve and a running nose.

Additional evidence of heroin usage may be found if a search is made for a needle or hypodermic syringe, cotton ball, tourniquet string, rope, belt, burnt bottle caps or spoons and glassine envelopes.

symptoms of heroin usage

Rathod, N. H., R. de Alarcon and I. G. Thomson. "Signs of Heroin Usage Detected by Drug Users and Their Parents," Lancet, 2: 1411–1414 (No. 7531), December 30, 1967.

Three physicians of the Horsham Psychiatric Service of St. Christopher's Day Hospital in Sussex, England report a study on how you can recognize that a person is taking heroin.

Twenty heroin users between the ages of 14 and 21 years

were asked to respond to a list of 38 possible signs; 20 parents of heroin addicts also cooperated in the study. The list of 38 possible signs of heroin use had been previously prepared by 12 heroin addicts and their parents who spontaneously described the observations or signs by which they were able to recognize that heroin users were under the influence of the drug.

The 20 leading signs of heroin use, as agreed upon by 50 per cent or more of addicts and parents were as follows:

sign of heroin use	Percentage of Recognition By Addict	By Parent
1. Wants to be left alone, may get very irritable	100	85
2. Looks dreamy and detached, seems far away	100	85
3. Does not want a proper meal	100	80
4. Blood spotting on clothes (pajama tops and shirts)	100	50
5. Slow and slurred speech	97	70
6. Cannot concentrate	93	75
7. Perspires	93	75
8. Rubbing of eyes, chin, and nasal areas	93	75
9. Fidgety with hands and paces up and down	93	70
10. Scratches arms and legs and areas where clothes rub	93	65
11. Unexpected absences from home (to obtain supply of heroin)	93	65

12.	Sleeps out, loses motivation	93	65
13.	Resents being disturbed or spoken to; avoids noise	93	65
14.	Wakefulness interrupted by absences or drowsiness	93	65
15.	Receives and makes frequent telephone calls (to check on supplies)	93	55
16.	Posture very relaxed; lies down	87	80
17.	Does not want to eat	87	70
18.	Gives up organized activities	87	60
19.	Wide open and glazed eyes	80	80
20.	May go to the toilet to vomit	73	70

heroin users in the identification of other addicts

Alarcon, R. de and N. H. Rathod. "Prevalence and Early Detection of Heroin Abuse," British Medical Journal, 2: 549-553, June 1, 1968.

Two English psychiatrists, in discussing the early detection of heroin users in young people, contend that from their studies one of the most effective ways of finding other addicts is to ask those who come for help because of complications from their abuse of the drug.

In a study that detected 98 users of heroin, the identifications of 46 came from addicts undergoing treatment and 20 identifications resulted from the development of jaundice as a result of complications from heroin injections that resulted in the addicts going to physicians. Police and probation officers combined were able to identify only nine users of heroin, physicians identified eight others (exclusive of jaundice) and 15 were found because of complications from amphetamines or barbiturates. The investigators were able to confirm in 50 cases that the subjects did indeed use heroin.

None of the foregoing identification, or screening methods, were judged to be ideal, but they did reveal that routine methods of detection of the heroin addict does not come soon enough, and that the addict under treatment can be a dependable source for the location of other heroin users who may need treatment also.

nalorphine (nalline) test for heroin

Elliott, Henry W., Norman Nomof, Kenneth Parker, Marjorie L. Dewey and E. Leong Way. "Comparison of the nalorphine test and urinary analysis in the detection of narcotic use," Clinical Pharmacology and Therapeutics, 5: 405–413, July-August 1964.

Five investigators of the Hine Laboratories and San Francisco Medical Center report a study of the value of the nalorphine (Nalline) test and the use of chemical tests of the urine for the identification of narcotics users.

The nalorphine (Nalline) test has been known for more than 15 years as a means of testing for narcotic addiction at low cost. Nalorphine is a narcotic antagonist that acts in an opposite manner than that of heroin, morphine, and associated drugs in terms of pupil size. Heroin, for example, causes an average constriction of the pupils of the eyes of about one-and-a-half millimeters two hours after the drug has been taken, according to these investigators.

Nalorphine (Nalline) was found to cause an expansion of the pupil that was most reliable within two to four hours after a drug has been taken. By 18 hours most of the subjects tested gave negative results. The narcotic antagonist did not appear to be reliable in detecting the intake of codeine, even when tried for a period of five days. However, after a single dose of morphine the nalorphine test was found to be positive in most addicts for four to six hours, but to be of no value for codeine detection. Positive tests occurred in the case of heroin two hours after the drug had been taken.

Chemical tests of the urine proved to be accurate in detecting an intake of morphine for as long as 36 hours. At 12 hours all the urine tests were positive, even when the nalorphine test was negative. Thus, the researchers advocate a combined use of chemical tests of the urine and the nalorphine test for identification of narcotics users.

pupil test for heroin and opium addiction

Way, E. Leong., Benjamin P. N. Mo, Collin P. Quock, P. M. Yap, George Ou, S. C. Chan and Jay Cheng. "Evaluation of the nalorphine pupil diagnostic test for narcotic usage in long-term heroin and opium addicts," Clinical Pharmacology and Therapeutics, 7: 300–311, May–June 1966.

A team of seven physicians and pharmacologists from California and Hong Kong report a study of the accuracy and reliability of the nalorphine test for heroin and opium addiction in 67 confirmed heroin users and 12 opium addicts.

All 79 of the Chinese adult male addicts had their addictions confirmed by urinary analysis with chemical tests.

The investigators found that the nalorphine test resulted in a reversal of the pupil constriction caused by the use of heroin or opium. The expansion of the pupils caused by the narcotic antagonist was most apparent within one to four hours and identification in this manner of the addict occurred in 95 per cent of the subjects. After this length of time there was a gradual decrease in the accuracy of the pupil test, although 22 per cent of the addicts still reacted with a positive response at 72 hours.

The pupil test was judged to be a helpful factor in diagnosis, but the researchers felt that it should not be used alone as evidence of narcotic usage. Signs on the addict such as needle marks, scars, abscesses, and withdrawal reactions should be looked for and whenever possible chemical tests of the urine should be made also. The advantages of the nalorphine test are speed, ease, convenience, and low cost.

No special laboratory facilities are needed and an answer can usually be obtained within about 30 minutes, and as many as 30 subjects can be tested within an hour.

detection of heroin addiction by
urine analysis

Marks, Vincent, Denys Fry, P. A. L. Chapple and Geoffrey Gray. "Application of Urine Analysis to Diagnosis and Treatment of Heroin Addiction," British Medical Journal, 1: 153-155, April 19, 1969.

Two English physicians in collaboration with two chemists report a study of 310 persons who were using heroin, or who were suspected of using it, by means of urine analysis.

The urine analysis technique used involved the color identification (chromatography) of morphine, since heroin is rapidly converted to morphine in the body and is not normally excreted in the urine even after rapid intravenous injection, except in the form of the latter drug.

Chromatography involves the identification by color of products contained in a liquid or gas, in this case urine. This scientific technique can identify morphine in concentrations as low as one microgram in a milliliter of urine.

Absence of morphine from the urine is not conclusive proof that heroin has not been taken. A negative result may mean only that less than 10 milligrams of heroin have been taken in the past 24 hours. The presence of morphine in the urine may mean the person has taken either morphine or heroin, or even codeine. The latter drug, however, will also be present in the urine in large amounts, even if certain morphine compounds from codeine are also present; so that codeine addiction can be distinguished by urine tests from morphine or heroin addiction.

From their studies of the 310 subjects the investigators concluded that thin-layer chromatography is valuable in detecting drug abuse. Results of the test can be available within five to 24 hours. A negative result means that the subject has taken less than 10 milligrams of heroin within the preceding 24 hours. [Another authority points out that results of the test are rarely available within five to 24 hours.—Ed.]

detection of addict babies in san francisco

Sussman, Sidney. "Narcotic and Methamphetamine Use During Pregnancy," American Journal of Diseases of Children, 106: 125–130, September 1963.

A physician of the University of California Medical Center and San Francisco General Hospital reports his observations of 19 addict mothers and their babies.

Twelve of the addict mothers used heroin alone during their pregnancies, but three others used both heroin and codeine. The remaining four maternal addicts used codeine and barbiturates, methamphetamine, marijuana, or some unknown drug.

Seventeen of the babies had withdrawal symptoms and 11 of them had difficulty in breathing. Some of the withdrawal symptoms were vague and insignificant, but others were more striking, such as convulsions, hyperactivity, tremors, excessive irritability, shrill crying, yawning and sneezing.

A history of addiction on the part of the mother, scarred veins, or withdrawal symptoms on her part may help the physician diagnose addiction in the infant. Venereal disease, liver infection, blood infections, blood clots and illegitimacy may also indicate the likelihood of drug addiction on the part of both mother and infant [as may a urine chromatography test—Ed.].

Sedatives and narcotic drugs must be used sparingly with addict babies as their ability to breathe may be further depressed. Mild withdrawal symptoms can be handled without any kind of drug treatment, according to Dr. Sussman, who reports that in his experience few addict babies have been seen who needed any kind of drug treatment.

Newborn infants do not have a psychic dependence on drugs. In a follow-up study of 10 infants Dr. Sussman found normal mental and physical development in nine and mental retardation in one.

evidence of heroin in the blood

Nakamura, George R. and Tyunosin Ukita. "Paper Chromatography Study of In Vitro and In Vivo Hydrolysis of Heroin in Blood," Journal of Pharmacological Science, 56: 294–295, February 1967.

Two Japanese scientists, one a member of the Faculty of Pharmaceutical Sciences of the University of Tokyo, report a study of the length of time that some evidence of heroin abuse will remain in the blood.

Diacetylmorphine hydrochloride (heroin) was added to a fresh sample of human blood serum and submitted to various technical laboratory tests. In addition, heroin was injected intramuscularly into three dogs, after which blood samples were taken every 10 minutes and tested for evidence of heroin residuals.

The studies showed that the principal breakdown product of heroin (diacetylmorphine hydrochloride) in the blood was monoacetylmorphine and that when heroin entered the blood it was rapidly reduced to this simpler chemical compound. The detection of this substance (monoacetylmorphine) in the blood was judged to be legal evidence of the prior usage of heroin by the investigators.

It was found that evidence of heroin intake persists for at least seven hours, but that the blood sample should be taken within half an hour after the intake of heroin for proper preservation and preparation. [Samples are infrequently available on this schedule in actual practice, for obvious reasons.—Ed.]

The research investigators considered blood evidence of heroin usage as stronger legal evidence than findings in the urine.

heroin and the swelling of lung tissues

Lynch, Kenneth, Edward Greenbaum and B. J. O'Loughlin. "Pulmonary Edema in Heroin Overdose," Radiology, 94: 377–378, February 1970.

Three physicians of the University of California at Irvine and the West Valley Community Hospital at Encino say that edema of lung tissue has been found in up to 90 per cent of persons suffering from an acute overdosage of heroin.

The doctors believe that heroin addicts now outnumber morphine addicts by a ratio of 50 to 1 and that any young male who has swelling of the lung tissues without previous disease should be examined for the possibility of his being a heroin addict.

The physicians report a case study of a 21-year old male heroin addict whose parents found him in a coma with blue face and pink, frothy sputum. The patient had been released from a narcotics rehabilitation center only four days previously. On admission to the hospital his heart rate was 144 per minute and respiration 44 per minute. His pupils were constricted and needle marks were found in both arms. A chest film revealed his lung involvement and under proper medical treatment his breathing became normal within 24 hours, X-rays showed almost complete clearing of both lungs, and he was dismissed after 36 hours in the hospital.

Sometimes only one lung, or even one lobe of a lung, may be involved in the reaction to heroin and in these cases it may be difficult for the radiologist to distinguish the condition from pneumonia.

When disturbed respiration, stupor, and constricted pupils are observed in a patient the doctors believe a physician should be alerted to the possibility of narcotic overdosage.

It is not known exactly what causes the swelling of lung tissue from heroin overdosage, but theories suggest the damage may be caused by an increase in spinal fluid and intracranial pressure, a reduced sensitivity to carbon dioxide in the respiratory center in the brain that causes diminished ventilation and impairment of capillary permeability that allows fluid from blood vessels to enter the lung tissues, or some irritation of lung tissue directly that is followed by a widespread inflammatory reaction. It is not known if any of these theories is a correct one.

large skin blister as clue to heroin use

Katz, Seymour, Israel M. Stein and Milford Fulop. "Bullous Eruption Associated With Heroin Pulmonary Edema," Journal of the American Medical Association, 216: 145 (No. 1), April 5, 1971.

Three New York physicians report the case history of a heroin addict who was brought to the hospital in an unconscious state after being found in that condition at home. He was reported as having been in excellent health and at that time was not known to be a user of heroin.

At first it was thought the patient was suffering from an infection, but constricted pupils and other signs suggested the possibility of an overdose of heroin. Nalorphine (Nalline), a narcotic antagonist was given and the patient improved dramatically. Later that day he admitted to the doctors that he had given himself an injection of heroin.

On the second day of hospitalization, where redness and swelling of the skin had existed, large bullae (blisters) containing straw-colored fluid developed on the palm of the hand and the instep of a foot. High concentration of protein in the blister fluid suggested to the physicians that the capillaries of the area had been damaged and became more permeable so that leakage occurred from the blood into the bullae. The doctors also thought the same phenomenon might have explained, at least in part, the swelling of lung tissue that was also observed in the addict.

skin signs of heroin addiction

Mandy, Stephen and A. Bernard Ackerman. "Characteristic Traumatic Skin Lesions in Drug-Induced Coma," Journal of the American Medical Association, 213: 253–256, July 13, 1970.

Two physicians of the Department of Dermatology of the University of Miami School of Medicine in Florida report that the drug addict in a coma may have skin signs that reveal his addiction and may save his life if they are recognized by the attending physician.

The doctors report two cases of heroin addicts who were brought to the hospital in a coma. One of the victims was found by his wife in a coma with blisters over his wrists and ankles after "sniffing heroin" about 12 hours earlier. The other patient became combative in the hospital and restraints were placed on his wrists. Within moments large blisters appeared on the wrists and hands beneath the restraints.

The skin reactions were studied in detail by the physicians, in respect to the skin itself and the fluid the blisters contained. Nearby normal skin was also studied. It was found the disorder developed first as a dark, reddish patch on the skin, with blisters appearing within minutes in areas where friction or stress was present. In both patients there was extensive death of the skin tissue containing the sweat glands. Sweat ducts and the surrounding skin lost their normal qualities. Other changes were also noted.

Over 500 cases of blister development by drug addicts suffering from overdosage of a variety of different drugs have been noted in the medical literature by physicians, mostly by Europeans.

Recognition of reddish and blistering skin as a possible sign of drug overdosage by physicians may enable them to save the lives of some heroin or other drug addicts.

excessive breast development as a clue
to heroin addiction in males

Camiel, Mortimer R., Leslie L. Alexander and David L. Ben-
ninghoff. "Drug Addiction and Gynecomastia," New York
State Journal of Medicine, 67: 2494-2495, September 15,
1967.

Three physicians of Brooklyn, New York believe that there
are few clues to drug addiction in many addicts and that doctors may often miss the diagnosis.

In this report, a little-known sign of heroin addiction is
described in two addicts who had been using the drug for
eight and 10 years respectively. In both of the narcotics users
the breast was enlarged due to excessive development of the
mammary glands. One of the patients was admitted to the
hospital for jaundice and the other for plastic surgery on the
right breast.

Enlargement of the male breast is almost always a result of
an imbalance of hormones and in the patient with liver disease that resulted in jaundice (yellowish discoloration) it
could have been impairment of the normal functioning of the
liver that resulted in an inability to deactivate estrogen in the
blood. The doctors believe that whenever a male patient has
one or both breasts enlarged without an explanation the examining physician should take steps to see if narcotic addiction may be the source of the abnormality.

x-rays in the detection of heroin abuse

Stern, Wilhelm Z., Paul W. Spear, and Harold G. Jacobson. "The Roentgen Findings in Acute Heroin Intoxication," American Journal of Roentgenology, Radium Therapy and Nuclear Medicine, 103: 522-532, July 1968.

Although the diagnosis of an acute overdosage of heroin can be made from clinical symptoms and signs as well as from blood studies, any additional evidence that alerts the physician to a correct diagnosis is valuable because of the urgent need for proper treatment.

Three radiologists of the Albert Einstein College of Medicine report, from their experience with 15 addicts suffering from severe reactions to an overdosage of heroin, that X-rays are very useful in helping the physician to arrive at a correct interpretation of the patient's immediate problem and its severity.

Chest X-rays of the 15 addicts showed marked changes in the lungs ranging from a diffuse swelling to pneumonia, lung abscess, and lung collapse with fluid in and around the lung tissues.

With proper medical treatment with narcotic antagonists, X-ray evidence of lung damage began to disappear within 24 hours with some patients, but in others it took as long as six weeks for the lungs to return to a normal appearance under X-rays. Two of the heroin users in this study died with massive changes in the lungs, but 13 others recovered under treatment.

X-rays revealed evidence of heroin addiction in other parts of the body, as, for example, at the sites of injection of the drug, where broken needle fragments were sometimes found, as well as abscesses outside the lungs.

X-rays give clear evidence that the swelling of lung tissues is one of the effects of heroin overdosage that impairs effective respiration, which, superimposed on the depressant effects of heroin on the brain, may cause death from respiratory failure.

6

effects associated with heroin

addiction

There are many undesirable medical effects of addiction to heroin and many of them are concerned not with the drug itself, but with the circumstances that surround its use. If the addict does not secure his drug on schedule he suffers from withdrawal symptoms. If he takes too much of the drug he may kill himself. These effects are discussed in the next two chapters. In this chapter a variety of the results of heroin addiction are considered even though they do not represent the total picture of harmful events.

Individual sensitivities, varying contaminants, different dosages, pre-existing levels of health, and various degrees of understanding make each injection of heroin an unpredictable experience for each addict. Most heroin users are notoriously ignorant, careless, or indifferent to the hazards of infection and a variety of contagious diseases are apt to afflict them. Many disorders of addicts are directly related to substances with which heroin is contaminated, but which may be sources of profound shock, injury to some part of the body, or even death.

the major medical complications of
heroin abuse

Labi, Moshe. "Paroxysmal Atrial Fibrillation in Heroin Intoxication," Annals of Internal Medicine, 71: 951–959, November 1969.

A member of the Albert Einstein College of Medicine and the Lincoln Hospital in the Bronx says the major medical complications of heroin use are: 1) respiratory depression; 2) infection of the inner lining of the heart (endocarditis); 3) swelling of lung tissue; 4) blood clots from dead tissue that lodge in the lungs; 5) high blood pressure that results from foreign body reactions of abnormal tissue; 6) liver disease; 7) tetanus; 8) skin abscesses; 9) inflammation and infection of blood vessels with formation of blood clots, and 10) the presence of bacteria in the blood.

The Bronx physician adds another complication that may occur in heroin addiction: abnormal rhythm of the upper chambers of the heart (atrial fibrillation). During the year prior to this report Dr. Labi and his associates treated 60 patients for heroin intoxication. Six, or 10 per cent, had transient atrial fibrillation.

All of the six patients were in a coma and blue in the face. Five had severe respiratory depression. Electrocardiograms were taken of four of the patients before treatment was begun and all had abnormality of rhythm of the upper heart chambers. Two who had ECG's taken after treatment was started also showed fibrillation. The doctor believes that the disturbance of heart rhythm found in his six heroin patients means many doctors overlook the possibility of such an occurrence, rather than that it is a rare condition.

complications from heroin

Louria, Donald B., Terry Hensle, and John Rose. "The Major Medical Complications of Heroin Addiction," Annals of Internal Medicine, 67: 1–22, July 1967.

A national authority on drug abuse and two research associates of the Cornell University Medical College report that although an overdosage of heroin causes the most deaths of addicts there are also other medical complications from the use of this drug.

The Cornell research team analyzed 100 complications and reactions from the use of heroin and found that overdosage reactions, inflammation of the heart, lung disorders, inflammation of the liver (hepatitis), tetanus, blood clots, abscesses at the point of injection, inflammation of blood vessels and infections of various cells and tissues of the body are the leading medical complications that are observed today by physicians. Malaria, due to the use of unsterile needles by addicts who have shared them with users infected with the disease, had not occurred at the time of this report in the United States due to its eradication in this country.

The doctors report that any mixture that contains more than 20 per cent heroin may cause death from overdosage and that physicians should suspect heroin as a cause whenever they observe a patient in a stuporous condition who is having difficulty breathing and whose lungs are congested.

Since no addict can ever be completely sure of how much heroin he is buying on the illegal market it is not surprising that about one in every 100 users of this drug dies annually, according to the Cornell investigators.

Infections of the inner lining of the heart appear to be especially hazardous to the heroin addict. Of 48 addicts in the study who had this condition only 15 recovered.

Liver infections from the sharing of unsterile needles may cause lasting damage, even after apparent recovery and discharge from the hospital. Addicts who leave the hospital before recovery are likely to have abnormal livers for longer periods of time.

Tetanus from the use of unsterile needles still occurs in heroin addicts. At Bellevue Hospital in New York City about two cases of this disease are admitted each year because of the injection of heroin.

The lungs may be damaged by the swelling of respiratory tissues, formation of abscesses, lodging of blood clots from other parts of the body, development of pneumonia and partial or complete paralysis of respiration from an overdosage.

medical complications of heroin abuse

Louria, Donald B. "Medical Complications of Pleasure-Giving Drugs," Archives of Internal Medicine, 123: 82–87, January 1969.

A physician of the Cornell University Medical College in New York City says that heroin is so flagrantly adulterated that the addict admitted to a hospital for withdrawal or some medical treatment can usually be treated with mild sedation without resort to substitute narcotics such as methadone.

Often, illicit heroin is so weak and adulterated that the addict uses some other drug in combination with it, such as a barbiturate or amphetamine. If the second drug is a stimulant it may mask the heroin. If it is a barbiturate the dual addiction must be recognized or withdrawal may cause an occasional death.

Dr. Louria identifies the major medical complications of addiction to heroin as: 1) abscesses and pus-containing infections of the skin; 2) infections of the inner lining of the heart; 3) liver disease; 4) an overdosage of heroin; 5) pneumonia; 6) infected blood clots in the lungs; 7) tetanus, and 8) inflammation and infections of blood vessels with the formation of clotted blood at the site.

At the Bellevue Hospital in New York City an overdosage of heroin is seen most frequently as a consequence of heroin addiction. It is now the leading cause of death in the age group of 15 to 35 years. In persons dying of an overdose of heroin the signs are apt to be constricted pupils, needle marks, slow breathing, fever, and acute congestion of the lungs. A major problem with addicts who suffer from an overdose of heroin is that they may never reach the hospital, but will be found dead in an alley or some slovenly room, or may recover spontaneously with help from friends.

One complication from the use of heroin is seldom seen today. It is the perforation of the nasal septum as a result of sniffing heroin or cocaine.

lack of cleanliness of heroin addicts
linked to infections

Merry, Julius and B. M. Gompels. "Miliary Tuberculosis, Tuberculosis of Ribs and Heroin Addiction," British Journal of Psychiatry, 116: 645-646, June 1970.

Two staff members of the St. Thomas Hospitals in London report that British drug addicts are notorious for their lack of cleanliness and precautions against infection when they inject heroin. Even the most elementary hygienic precautions are neglected. Dirty needles and syringes are used, often in sequence by different addicts. Unboiled tap water may be used to dissolve heroin for use and even water from a toilet has been used. Addicts may not even clean the skin and in desperate moments may even inject themselves through several layers of clothing.

A case report is given of a 31-year old Canadian who had used heroin and cocaine for eight years, who came to a Drug Dependence Unit for his daily dosage of drugs. He came to the clinic with an infected ulcer in his right arm and a complaint of "flu" along with pains in his chest and a cough, but resisted the idea of going to a hospital. Later he complained of chest pains on both sides and tender lumps on the chest wall. The lumps on the chest wall were drained of pus and bacteriological studies led to a diagnosis of tuberculosis of the ribs. He was treated in the hospital with antituberculosis drugs and discharged in reasonably good condition.

On questioning the addict admitted that he sometimes borrowed needles for self-injection of heroin from other addicts and said the latter sometimes cleaned the needles by licking them. It is probable that the infecting needle had been licked by another addict with open tuberculosis of the lungs (and tubercle bacilli in his saliva—Ed.).

infection hazards of injection techniques

Bewley, Thomas H., Oved Ben-Arie and Vincent Marks, "Relation of Hepatitis to Self-injection Techniques," British Medical Journal, 1: 730–732, March 23, 1968.

Three English doctors report a study of the injection techniques of 50 heroin addicts in an effort to find the reasons for the high incidence of liver disease that they had observed in patients under their treatment in London.

Needles and syringes were carried in an unsterile and careless manner by 11 addicts, so that contamination could easily occur.

Twenty-seven of the patients dissolved heroin in cold tap water; sterile water was declared to be too expensive. Fifteen of the addicts had at one time or another dissolved heroin in water drawn from lavatory pans (toilets or urinals). Only six addicts regularly dissolved the drug by boiling or "cooking" it.

Syringes were used frequently, for weeks or months, until broken or lost. The syringes were used from twice to six times daily over the periods of time noted. Not one single addict used a syringe once only.

Needles were used over and over again. Although 30 addicts used disposable needles they did not get rid of them after use, but used them over and over again. Nineteen addicts used all-steel needles and even sharpened blunt needles on "a kitchen sink or steps." Only one addict professed to use a new, clean and sterile needle each time.

Cleaning of injection equipment was poorly done. Syringes were flushed only if they were noticeably dirty. Four addicts never cleaned their equipment. Twenty-three addicts flushed their syringes with cold water, seven with hot tap water and five with some antiseptic solution after use. Six patients had injected old blood clots inside their syringes and one addict said he injected "more tobacco and dust than heroin."

Boiling of instruments between injections was not done by even one addict on a regular basis, and 31 addicts who used disposable equipment never boiled it.

General cleanliness was poor. Fifteen of the addicts never cleaned their skin before injecting heroin. Ten felt needles with their fingers to detect blunt ones, eight had blown through the needle when it was blocked. Six licked blood off their skin after injection. Five had put equipment on the floor before use, often in toilets. Most of the addicts knew about the dangers of intravenous injections, but chose to ignore them.

drugs and disease

Francisco, J. T. *"Drugs and Disease—A Pathologist's Viewpoint," Journal of Forensic Sciences, 10: 407–414, October 15, 1965.*

A physician of the Institute of Pathology of the University of Tennessee in Memphis observes that with the increasing use of drugs the scientist must be aware that drugs can cause disease.

This medical pathologist observes that drug overdosage has been recognized ever since drugs have been used as a cure for disease. For many drugs the signs of overdosage are not immediately recognized by doctors. When death occurs the pathologist may find in autopsy studies that there is an extreme accumulation of fat in the liver. In overdosage with some drugs the kidneys may fail and autopsy findings confirm the dause of death in disturbed kidney cells.

Some persons may be born with enzyme system deficiencies that are not revealed until tissue injuries occur from commonly used drugs that are given within the recommended levels. In such people the enzyme systems cannot properly handle the drugs with which other persons have no difficulties. Many drugs may cause the red blood cells to be destroyed and the hemoglobin released may damage the kidneys, possibly by blocking the tubules of the latter.

All drugs have primary and secondary effects. Sometimes the secondary, or side reactions, are slow to be recognized. Only recently has aspirin (acetylsalicylic acid) been recognized as a cause of bleeding from the stomach.

Many drugs cause allergic or hypersensitivity reactions.

One of the most serious effects is on the blood-forming organs, so that a severe anemia may develop. Effects on the bone marrow, where red blood cells are produced, may be so damaging that there is a cessation of blood formation.

Doctor Francisco observes that although drugs are a definite blessing to medicine, there is a danger to every drug so that the cure for today's disease may be the cause of tomorrow's death.

severe infections in heroin addicts

Briggs, J. H., C. G. McKerron, R. L. Souhami, D. J. E. Taylor and Hilary Andrews. "Severe Systemic Infections Complicating 'Mainline' Heroin Addiction," The Lancet, 2: 1227–1231, December 9, 1967.

Five London physicians report that since 1961 the number of young people in England who are addicted to heroin and cocaine has risen sharply and that severe generalized infections often complicate the use of these drugs.

The doctors report their experiences with 11 young, unemployed heroin and cocaine addicts who were admitted to London hospitals with chest infections and bacteria in the blood. When admitted all of the addicts had fever and respiratory disease. Most had infections at sites of injection, abscesses of the skin, or infected, pus-producing infections of blood vessels.

Two of the patients died with severe infection and circulatory collapse. Four others suffered from severe blood infection and acute arthritis. The remaining five patients had acute pneumonia and staphylococci were found in the blood.

As a group the heroin addicts were emaciated and had a variety of complications including a severe toxic condition and a cough. At first X-ray films of the chest showed little, but later showed more disease of the chest and at autopsy multiple lung abscesses, hemorrhages and blood clots were found in the lungs.

The patients who died did so despite intensive medical treatment. The high doses of heroin the young English addicts were taking were judged by the physicians to be the source of the emaciation, weakness, and susceptibility to severe and overwhelming infections that they showed.

infected addicts in new york differ from those in england

Cherubin, Charles E. and Jacqueline Brown. "Systemic Infections in Heroin Addicts," The Lancet, 1: 298–299, February 10, 1968.

Two staff members of the Harlem Hospital Center in New York say that symptoms ascribed to 11 young English heroin addicts who had severe pulmonary infections are in many ways similar to those of New York City addicts, but that certain differences should be noted.

In New York 13 heroin addicts with lung infections responded readily to penicillin. Complicated cases with disease germs in the blood and abscess formation were in the minority. The New York addicts are not emaciated. The emacia-

tion of the English addicts may be due to the ease with
which they obtain heroin of such purity by medical prescription that the drug suppresses their desire for food. Infected
blood clots from the lungs do not seem to be a factor in the
New York addicts, perhaps because of the absence of infected blood vessels in the patients observed.

Of 28 heroin addicts admitted to the Harlem Hospital
Center with infections of the inner lining of the heart, one-
third had a history of pneumonia. However, less than five per
cent of the addicts who enter with pneumonia have some
other diagnosis as well.

The two physicians also wonder about tetanus in English
addicts. In New York the doctors say the risk of tetanus in
heroin users is very great, despite the fact that many addicts
are immunized against the disease.

staphylococcus infections of the heart

*Olsson, Ray A. and Monroe J. Romansky. "Staphylococcal
Tricuspid Endocarditis in Heroin Addicts," Annals of Internal Medicine, 57: 755–762, November 1962.*

Two physicians of the George Washington University School
of Medicine observe that infection of the inner lining of the
heart is a complication of heroin addiction, especially in addicts who use the intravenous route for drug taking.

The doctors report six patients who were heroin addicts,
all of whom were found to have staphylococcus infections
of the lining of the heart and valves with arterial blood clots
in the lungs, eyes, and kidneys. Because of the appearance of

the lungs on X-ray examination which suggested long standing damage, the doctors thought it possible that the blood clots had originated in the lungs rather than from the heart valves. In one patient who died numerous micro-abscesses were found in the kidneys that were similar to findings in other autopsies where the valves of the heart had been damaged.

The tricuspid valve of the heart was involved in all six cases and the two physicians believe that heroin injection, staphylococcus infection, and tricuspid valve damage should be linked as a triad.

infection of the inner lining of the heart

Thompson, William R. "H vaginicola Endocarditis in a Heroin Addict," Journal of the American Medical Association, 215: 982, February 8, 1971.

An Atlantic City physician calls attention to studies that indicate inflammation of the inner lining of the heart from infections and death of tissue have caused about eight per cent of the deaths of narcotic addicts in New York City over a period of years.

Although most disease organisms that cause infections of the heart are well known to doctors, this physician reports the case of a 32-year old heroin addict who died 28 days after being admitted to the hospital. A blood specimen yielded a pure culture of H vaginicola, an organism that is usually found in patients with wounds, burns, and malignant tumors. Autopsy of the heart showed that the aortic valve was two-thirds destroyed and damage had been done to the remaining parts of the valve. Areas of dead tissue due to circulatory obstruction were found in the spleen, kidneys, and brain; they were probably due to clots or fragments from the diseased heart.

heroin and diminished functioning of the lungs

Gelfand, Maxwell L., Henry Hammer and Theodore Hevizy. "Asymptomatic Pulmonary Atelectasis in Drug Addicts," Diseases of the Chest, 52: 782–787, December 1967.

Three physicians of the Beth Israel Medical Center in New York City report that chest X-ray films of many drug addicts admitted to the hospital show lung damage without clinical symptoms of respiratory distress.

A study of 10 men and four women who had been addicted to heroin for one to 30 years showed that they were given careful X-ray examinations to assess the status of the lungs. None of the addicts had a cough, fever, difficult breathing, chest pains or previous history of lung disease. None had coughed up blood from the lungs.

The X-rays showed incomplete expansion of lung tissue and a shrinking of lung spaces with implications of a lung that is not functioning in a normal manner, but only a small segment of the lung was affected. The foregoing condition (atelectasis) is secondary to some other disease or damaging process, such as an infection, inflammation, pain on respiration or other condition. The symptoms of the disorder may vary from none at all to difficult breathing, rapid, shallow breathing, cough and blueness.

The 14 addicts of this study showed the above X-ray evidence of impaired lung function while under the influence of heroin although there were no clinical signs of distress.

swelling of lung tissue from heroin

Steinberg, Alfred D. and Joel S. Karlinger. "The Clinical Spectrum of Heroin Pulmonary Edema," Archives of Internal Medicine, 122: 122-127, August 1968.

Two physicians of the Albert Einstein College of Medicine and the Bronx Municipal Hospital Center report a study of 16 heroin addicts who were hospitalized because of emergency conditions involving coma and respiratory distress. Fourteen of the patients lapsed into a coma and most had difficulty in breathing. Only two patients seemed to be breathing normally when they were first seen by the doctors.

Because lung congestion and swelling may get progressively worse and go into pneumonia within 24 hours, the doctors believe that all patients suspected of reacting to an overdose of heroin should be kept in the hospital for observation for at least 24 hours before being sent home. Severe lung congestion may even develop several hours after recovery from coma has occurred.

Twelve of the patients in this study were treated with nalorphine (Nalline) a narcotic antagonist and seven of the patients needed placement of a tube in the throat to assist breathing. Other treatment included the use of antibiotics and positive pressure ventilation with oxygen. A few patients needed other medicines, including digitalis to strengthen the heart and steroids to control inflammation.

Fourteen of the patients recovered completely, 12 of them within five days. Seven were well within 48 hours. Two of the patients died, one with irreversible brain damage from a lack of oxygen and several cardiac arrests. The other patient was found dead in bed 16 hours after admission, with his lungs full of frothy congestion and an enlarged heart. His kidneys, liver, spleen, adrenal glands and brain were also swollen. His severe pneumonia was thought to be a major factor in his death.

swollen lungs from heroin

Selzman, Harold M., Michel E. Kahil and Herbert L. Fred. "Pulmonary Edema Accompanying Heroin Intoxication," Cardiovascular Research Center Bulletin, 6: 77–79, October-December 1967.

Three physicians of Baylor University College of Medicine in Houston observe that the swelling of lung tissue after heroin intoxication is a common finding at autopsy. The condition may occur also in non-fatal reactions to an overdose of heroin.

The authors report the case of a 25-year old man who was found unconscious in a parking lot with a strong odor of alcohol on his breath. However, needle marks were found on his arm and his pupils were constricted. He was treated with a narcotic antagonist and improved to the point that in three days he was discharged without symptoms.

In the meantime, however, he first denied and then admitted that he had taken his first injection of heroin. On admission to the hospital, in addition to his other symptoms, the patient showed lung congestion with a fast pulse and shallow, rapid breathing. The combination of coma, constricted pupils and needle marks convinced the physicians that his shallow, rapid breathing and swelling of lung tissues were all a reaction to heroin.

swelling of the lungs from heroin overdosage

Karliner, Joel S., Alfred D. Steinberg and M. Henry Williams. "Lung Function After Pulmonary Edema Associated With Heroin Overdose," Archives of Internal Medicine, 124: 350-353, September 1969.

Three physicians of the Albert Einstein College of Medicine and the Bronx Municipal Hospital Center observe that pulmonary edema (swelling of lung tissue) is a well recognized result from heroin overdosage and it may contribute to the death of the addict.

Lung congestion may begin rapidly or as long as 24 hours after the overdose. Sometimes the diagnosis can be made only by X-ray evidence. At other times the patient may be seriously ill or dying. Most patients do recover when oxygen is forced into their lungs for a period of time.

In this research five patients were studied for two to 12 days after having swelling of lung tissues from a heroin overdosage from which they had apparently recovered after medical treatment and from which they no longer had symptoms. The study revealed that vital capacity and total lung capacity had been reduced to only 49 and 56 per cent of normal expectancy. In other words, the lung tissues had been damaged and the physicians concluded that the five heroin patients may suffer from chronic lung disease short of normal functioning, even if no clinical signs of lung disease appear.

liver infections from heroin

Dismukes, William E., Adolf W. Karchmer, Ronald F. Johnson and William J. Dougherty. "Viral Hepatitis Associated With Illicit Parenteral Use of Drugs," Journal of the American Medical Association, 206: 1048–1052, October 28, 1968.

Heroin, in itself, cannot cause an infection of the liver. However, the manner in which heroin is injected can very definitely be a source of inflammation of the liver because of unsterile needles and exposure to the diseases of other addicts.

In this study four doctors of the National Communicable Disease Center report their experience and observations on the relationship of liver infections to drug abuse. The medical investigators found a strong association between the use of narcotics and virus infections of the liver.

The research team found evidence that the sharing of injection equipment among heroin addicts was a major factor in the spread of liver infections.

Many more virus infections of the liver may be due to the injection of drugs, since 63 per cent of the doctors in New Jersey, where this study was conducted, have admitted that they are reluctant to report narcotic offenders to police or health authorities.

It is certainly evident from this study and from others that the liver, one of the vital organs of the body without which life cannot survive, may be seriously damaged by drug addiction, especially with drugs that need to be injected into the body.

epidemic of liver disease in narcotic addicts

Rosenstein, Beryl J. "Viral Hepatitis in Narcotics Users," Journal of the American Medical Association, 199: 698–700, March 6, 1967.

A physician of the Rhode Island Department of Health reports that an epidemic of liver disease occurred in the Providence area that involved at least 27 patients who were injecting narcotics. Seven of the addicts had used heroin only, eight had used heroin with one or more other drugs and others had injected other drugs or refused to give information.

Twenty-one of the patients admitted using drugs with an addict who was jaundiced and most were members of one "ring" of drug users. Among the addicts who shared needles there were ineffective methods used to sterilize them, such as rinsing in tap water or alcohol.

It is likely that the epidemic was much larger as many of the patients reported other addicts were jaundiced but afraid to report for medical attention. One important aspect of the epidemic was the fact 41 per cent of the patients with jaundice were not at first recognized as drug addicts who were injecting drugs.

brain and nerve damage from
heroin addiction

Richter, Ralph W. and Michael M. Baden. "Neurological Complications of Heroin Addiction," American Neurological Association, 94: 330–332, 1969.

Two members of the staff of Harlem Hospital in New York City report on the effects of heroin addiction on the brain and nervous system as observed in 568 patients. Although many of the diagnoses of injury to nerve tissue were based on clinical observations by the neurologists, autopsy findings on addicts who died confirmed their judgments.

Inflammation of the spinal cord in the chest area was observed in seven addicts. After taking heroin five of the addicts became suddenly partially paralyzed. In one of the addicts who died extensive death of nerve tissue in the spinal cord was found. Another patient died, but the spinal cord was not examined after death. In two of the surviving patients a permanent partial paralysis has persisted. Hypersensitivity (allergic) reactions, impairment of the blood supply because of low blood pressure, a severe reaction to heroin or to some contaminant such as quinine were possible causes of the inflammation of nerve tissue.

Damage to individual nerves in the areas of injection, especially in the arms, resulted in permanent injury. Deep abscesses, chronic inflammation of cells and inflammation of blood vessels were all found to be followed by nerve damage. Inflammation of nerve tissue and burning, painful sensations due to nerve injury were found to occur in the heroin addicts, often in multiple nerves simultaneously.

Acute and chronic brain disorders were found in a large number of young heroin addicts. The patients were brought to the hospital unconscious, in a partial coma and with convulsions. Persistent mental changes associated with brain damage were observed in some of the surviving heroin users. One addict was unconscious after injecting heroin 14 hours previously. On awakening he showed mental changes and a tremor that persisted for two years. Two addicts who developed paralysis on one side of the body were found to be suffering from a blocking of a main brain artery by blood clots. Changes in brain functioning were found to occur with many severe infections traceable to the injection of heroin because of a lack of sterile precautions with the needle.

Death from tetanus occurred in eight of 12 heroin addicts suffering from this disease. The great majority of tetanus cases in New York City are now found to occur in heroin addicts. In three of the deaths the heart was found at autopsy to be damaged along with damage to the nervous system.

Numerous other damaging effects of heroin addiction were found at autopsy by the physicians.

death and paralysis from heroin injection

Richter, Ralph W. and Roger N. Rosenberg. "Transverse Myelitis Associated With Heroin Addiction," Journal of the American Medical Association, 206: 1255-1257, November 4, 1968.

Two neurologists of Columbia University and the Harlem Hospital Center report four cases in which heroin addicts showed paralysis shortly after injections of heroin. One patient died after taking heroin a second time five weeks later.

Autopsy studies of this victim showed extensive death of spinal cord tissue.

The mechanism that produced paralysis and death by damage to nerve tissue was not clear to the physicians. True allergic reactions can occur from heroin. [They can also be caused by adulterants.—Ed.] Heroin may depress the blood-pressure regulating center of the brain with alterations of blood supply to body tissues. The release of histamine after an injection of heroin may contribute also to a severe low blood pressure and reduction of circulation to some tissues. Quinine, frequently used with heroin, may likewise cause impairments of circulation. The rapid onset of paralysis within several hours after injection of heroin suggests an allergic or hypersensitive reaction as cause of the damage to the central nervous system in these patients.

paralysis from a heroin injection

Thompson, William R. and Morton B. Waldman. "Cervical Myelopathy Following Heroin Administration," Journal of the Medical Society of New Jersey, 67: 223-224, May 1970.

Two physicians of Atlantic City report the case of a 20-year old heroin addict who developed inflammation of the spinal cord in the neck region.

The addict fell to the floor immediately after injecting a bag of heroin into the right cephalic vein. He was found four hours later by his landlady with the needle still in the vein. His fingers and lower extremities were paralyzed. After being helped to bed he slept for six hours and was then taken to the hospital where he was found to be completely paralyzed in both legs. He was also unable to move any of his fingers. After medical treatment he had rapid improvement of his leg paralysis and was able to stand on the 10th day, but there was no improvement in his ability to move his fingers.

The doctors are skeptical of the patient's ability to achieve a complete recovery and concluded that the most likely explanation of his sudden paralysis was a hypersensitive (allergic) reaction to the heroin or some contaminating substance that it contained.

brain damage and death of heroin addicts
from injection of milk

Drenick, Ernst J. and Kenneth M. Younger. "Heroin Over-
dose Complicated by Intravenous Injection of Milk," Journal
of the American Medical Association, 213: 1687, September
7, 1970.

Two physicians of Los Angeles observe that a rumor [not a
rumor, but a myth—Ed.] among heroin addicts is that milk is
a substance that can overcome the ill effects of an overdosage
of heroin, despite the fact that if milk is injected into a vein
there may be catastrophic results.

The two doctors report the case of a 19-year old who had
drunk one-half pint of rum, eaten four to eight barbiturate tablets, and injected one "balloon" of heroin. He quickly
became lethargic and friends who became alarmed over his
deepening stupor decided to inject two syringes of milk as an
antidote. Immediately the patient became worse.

The patient was treated at an emergency hospital with the
narcotic antagonist nalorphine (Nalline) hydrochloride and a
respirator bag. He was transferred to the Veterans Administration Hospital where he arrived in a comatose condition
with pinpoint pupils, severe lung swelling and other evidence
of a critical condition. After appropriate medical treatment
he gradually recovered.

When told of the dangers of injecting milk into a vein the
addict held to the belief that milk works.

Two other physicians who heard of this case reported they

had similar patient addicts in whom milk had been injected. One ended with a permanently damaged brain, in a vegetable-like condition, and the other died.

fungus infection of the brain in a heroin addict

Hameroff, Stephen Barry, John W. Eckholdt and Richard Lindenberg. "Cerebral Phycomycosis in a Heroin Addict," Neurology, 20: 261–265 (No. 3), March 1970.

Three physicians of the University of Maryland School of Medicine in Baltimore report on the death of a 32-year old narcotics addict from a fungus infection of the brain.

The addict was in a local prison for heroin addiction when he suddenly became ill. After being examined in the prison hospital he was transferred to the University Hospital where the three physicians supervised his diagnosis and treatment. He was stuporous and unable to swallow. He had difficulty moving his right side and spoke in a slurred manner. Other signs of paralysis and brain involvement were noted also. On the third day in the hospital the victim became deeply stuporous and died the next day.

Autopsy revealed that the man's brain was badly swollen with areas in which hemorrhage had occurred. Parts of the brain were very soft with some dead tissue. The lungs were also swollen.

Fungus was found to be present in the brain and was identified as phycomycosis. Some of the small arteries of the brain were found to be stuffed with this fungus and in places it could be seen growing through the walls of the blood vessels into the surrounding brain tissues.

Both bacterial and fungal diseases have been frequently reported in the medical literature as one of the complications of drug addiction. The physicians in this particular case concluded that the infection had occurred from the injection of contaminated heroin into a blood vessel and that the fungus had been carried to the brain via the blood.

From the medical literature reviewed by the three doctors in connection with this case study, it appears that narcotic addicts are prone to develop fungus infections from a contaminated drug or from an unsterile needle.

skin complications from heroin

Minkin, Wilfred and Harvey J. Cohen. "Dermatologic Complications of Heroin Addiction," New England Journal of Medicine, 277: 473–475, August 31, 1967.

Two physicians of New York University School of Medicine point out that the conditions under which heroin is injected by addicts lend themselves to infections. The heroin may be contaminated, the skin may not be cleaned, the needle and syringe or medicine dropper may be contaminated with germs and often the equipment used for injections is apt to be used by others who have some disease that can be spread by injection.

Several skin signs are indications of possible heroin addiction, such as thickened, cord-like superficial veins, thickening and hardened spots in the skin and small scars of wasted-away skin. Abscesses of the skin have been reported as a most common complication.

In this study the physicians report their experience with three heroin addicts who developed solid little knots (nodules) from which ulcerations occurred. These skin injuries developed at the site of the heroin injection within several hours. All of the addicts had injected heroin under the skin rather than into a blood vessel. The nodules were reddish, warm and tender. Infectious organisms were recovered from the ulcerating material and all patients healed within several weeks after medical treatment that included the use of antibiotics.

The doctors believe the described nodules were not abscesses and they were unable to determine whether they resulted from heroin itself, some contaminating substance, or an individual hypersensitivity. However, they do feel that observation of such skin disorders may alert the examining physician to the possibility that his patient may be a heroin addict.

dimness of vision from heroin contaminant

Brust, John C. M. and Ralph W. Richter. "Quinine Ambly-opia Related to Heroin Addiction," Annals of Internal Medicine, 74: 84-86, January 1971.

Two physicians of the Department of Neurology of Columbia University College of Physicians and Surgeons observe that dimness of vision due to an overdosage of quinine is well known to the medical profession. The fact that quinine is now commonly combined with heroin raises the possibility of damage to vision of heroin addicts.

The doctors observe that quinine is a tissue poison and may affect the brain and other parts of the nervous system, the heart, muscles, kidney, blood, ear and the eye. Mild reactions to quinine may be expressed in temporary ringing of the ears, headache, nausea, and decrease in vision. With greater amounts of quinine the symptoms may be more severe and longer lasting with deafness, vomiting, diarrhea, blindness, confusion, delirium and even death from respiratory arrest. Reports of quinine blindness are commonplace. The victim becomes blind or nearly blind with or without other symptoms. Often there is visual blurring, loss of some color perception, increased sensitivity to light, inability to see well in the dark and other symptoms.

The New York physicians report the case of a 40-year old patient who had been using from four to eight bags of a mixture of heroin, quinine and lactose daily by injection. He had a severe loss of vision that had begun about five months before he came to the hospital. He lost the vision in one eye during a 12-day period when he was injecting 45 to 50 bags of heroin daily. With lower dosages of the drug his vision partly returned, but then deteriorated or improved according to the amount of heroin mixture being used.

Quinine poisoning of the retina of the eye was diagnosed. He was put on methadone containing no quinine and his vision improved. He finally went back to the injection of heroin that contained no quinine.

Quinine is used as an adulterant of heroin because of its bitter taste which disguises the dilution of heroin (which is also bitter). Dilution, of course, increases the profits of the drug pusher.

a surgical problem from heroin injection

Fromm, Stefan H. and Charles E. Lucas. "Obturator Bypass for Mycotic Aneurysm in the Drug Addict," Archives of Surgery, 100: 82–83, January 1970.

Two surgeons of Wayne State University School of Medicine and the Detroit General Hospital report five cases where patients had injected heroin into the femoral vein and had developed pain and swelling in the right groin (lower abdominal area) due to the presence of an abscess and an aneurysm (a pocket-like protrusion from the wall of a blood vessel) that resulted from their "main lining" of the drug.

The five patients were operated on with good results, except for one addict who lost a leg because an amputation was necessary.

The usual symptoms of heroin addicts with the foregoing complication are swollen, painful, and pulsating masses of relatively recent origin in the right side of the lower abdomen.

blood destruction from heroin
contamination

Medrano, Victor A. and Kouichi R. Tanaka. "Hemolysis from Heroin Injected Intravenously," Journal of the American Medical Association, 212: 1380 (No. 8), May 25, 1970.

Two physicians of the Harbor General Hospital in Torrance, California report the case of a 22-year old male who had injected heroin into himself four hours prior to admission to this facility. At another hospital he had already been treated with nalorphine, oxygen, and dextrose in water, while in a comatose state with pinpoint pupils.

When he came under the care of the above two physicians he was still in a comatose condition. He also had bruises about his face and multiple injection punctures on his arm. His pulse was 120 beats per minute and laboratory reports indicated serious destruction of red blood cells. Six hours after admission the patient was passing burgundy-colored urine which was positive for blood.

The doctors were unable to find a cause for the massive destruction of red blood cells, but it was concluded that some substance used as a filler for heroin, or else some contaminating substance, was responsible. So far as these physicians were aware, no previous episode of this kind had been reported, but they feel that this sort of possible reaction to intravenous injections by drug addicts should be kept in mind.

The patient remained in the hospital for nine days and when discharged still had a very low red blood cell condition.

menstrual abnormalities after heroin

Gaulden, E. C., D. C. Littlefield, O. E. Putoff and A. L. Seivert. "Menstrual Abnormalities Associated with Heroin Addiction," American Journal of Obstetrics and Gynecology, 90: 155–160, September 15, 1964.

Four staff members of the California Rehabilitation Center in Corona, California report that heroin affects the process of menstruation, probably through an effect on the pituitary gland, secondary to an influencing of some other region of the brain, possibly the hypothalamus.

It is well known that the pituitary gland releases a hormone that is related to ovulation. Various drugs can activate the release of this hormone or may block it.

In this investigation 74 female heroin addicts who took the drug daily and who were residing at the rehabilitation center reported that before becoming addicted to heroin they had normal menstrual cycles, with very few exceptions. After beginning to use heroin 65 per cent had abnormal menstrual cycles. When heroin was discontinued the menstrual process returned to normal in most of the women.

ten-year disturbance of menstruation

Stoffer, Sheldon S., Duane N. Tweeddale, M.D. and Joseph D. Sapira. "Secondary Amenorrhea Persisting after Cessation of Narcotic Addiction," Obstetrics and Gynecology, 33: 558-559, April 1969.

Three physicians of the Clinical Research Center of Lexington, Kentucky report that there is a high incidence of cessation of menstruation during narcotic drug addiction and that although there is apt to be a return to a normal cycle after withdrawal, one study has found that abnormalities persist for at least three months in 43 per cent of the patients.

The doctors report a case in which heroin caused cessation of menstruation over a period of 10 years. The case study involved a young girl whose menstrual periods began at the age of 11 years and who had normal cycles until she began taking heroin at the age of 15 years. At the time of this report she was 25 years old. Although imprisoned for a period of two years, with enforced withdrawal from narcotics, her menstrual periods did not return to normal. The addict had been a prostitute since the age of 16 years, never used contraceptives and had never been pregnant. [The single case is cited as an example, but not a statistically-significant sample of this population.—Ed.]

heroin versus morphine

Martin, W. R. and H. F. Fraser. "A Comparative Study of Physiological and Subjective Effects of Heroin and Morphine Administered Intravenously in Postaddicts," Journal of Pharmacology and Experimental Therapy, 133: 388–399, September 1961.

Two research scientists of the Addiction Research Center in Lexington, Kentucky observe that heroin is the narcotic most frequently abused by American addicts.

It is sometimes said that drug users addicted to both heroin and morphine cannot distinguish between the effects of the two drugs.

In this research 11 subjects serving sentences for violation of federal narcotic laws, all of whom had a long history of opiate abuse, volunteered for the study. Their reactions were tested with heroin, morphine, and a placebo (a substance containing neither heroin nor morphine). After injection, each subject identified the drug with high accuracy and expressed a preference for heroin. However, the addicts did not express a great preference for heroin.

Several patients developed an aversion to heroin and morphine and did not want to take the drug every day.

heroin and the relief of pain

Reichle, Claus W., Gene M. Smith, Joachim S. Gravenstein, Spyros G. Macris and Henry K. Beecher. "Comparative Analgesic Potency of Heroin and Morphine in Postoperative Patients," Journal of Pharmacological and Experimental Therapy, 136: 43–46, April 1962.

Five members of the Harvard Medical School observe that heroin has been banned in the United States because it is supposed to be severely addictive, but little research has been done on the effects of heroin when used for the medical treatment of non-addicts.

In this study 522 patients who had been operated upon were given morphine in an evaluation of pain relief, as compared to the amount of pain relief achieved at four different dosages of heroin.

It was found that heroin was approximately two to four times as potent as morphine with respect to the relief of moderate, severe, or very severe pain from postoperative wounds within a period of 150 minutes after injection of the drug. Some other studies have shown that heroin may be from four to eight times as powerful, but the present investigators felt that those results were based upon the production of brief stabs of pain on an experimental basis, rather than pain of a pathological nature from surgery as was measured in this research.

heroin and chronic coughing

Woolf, C. R. and A. Rosenberg. "The Cough Suppressant Effect of Heroin and Codeine: A Controlled Clinical Study," Canadian Medical Association Journal, 86: 810–812, May 5, 1962.

A physician and his research associate measured with a double blind research technique the effects of heroin as compared to codeine in the control of chronic coughing from bronchitis.

Fourteen patients were used in the investigation with heroin ranging in age from 39 to 74 years. Four had chronic bronchitis, six had bronchitis with emphysema, three had lung cancer and one had pulmonary fibrosis. All had long-lasting coughs.

Thirty patients with comparable conditions and persisting cough took part in the codeine experiments.

The study revealed that a simple cough suppressant when used alone, such as terpin hydrate, was nearly as good as syrup of codeine and was equal to the same remedy to which heroin had been added.

The researchers observe that the disadvantages of codeine should be weighed against its use, since such a small superiority was shown over the simple syrup as a cough suppressant.

deaths and illnesses of heroin addicts

Cherubin, Charles E. "The Medical Sequelae of Narcotic Addiction," Annals of Internal Medicine, 67: 23–33, July 1967.

Death rates for heroin addicts are much greater than for other persons, and overdosage causes approximately 50 to 90 per cent of their deaths, according to a New York physician. Swollen lungs that no longer function properly, depression of the respiratory system, allergic or hypersensitive reactions to adulterating substances added to heroin by the pushers and direct toxic effects of the drug are responsible for the majority of the deaths of addicts. About 90 per cent of the heroin users who develop tetanus from the use of unsterilized needles can be expected to die and those who develop heart infections have an even worse record, according to Dr. Cherubin. His study of the records in four hospitals was unable to validate the recovery of even one addict who survived his heart infection over a period of 15 years.

The physical illnesses of addicts have not received as much medical attention as the fatalities, but they are extensive, says the New York physician. He identifies skin abscesses, blood clots in the lungs and elsewhere, pneumonia, tuberculosis, liver infections and inflammations of blood vessels as some of the leading illnesses of heroin users. Other complications are indicated also.

deaths of heroin addicts

James, I. Pierce. "Suicide and Mortality Amongst Heroin Addicts in Britain," British Journal of Addiction, 62: 391–398, December 1967.

It is possible that many users of heroin become addicts because of problems and internal stresses that would dispose them to suicide and early deaths even if they had not resorted to the drug, but it is quite clear that a shortened life span and the use of heroin are related in direct ways as well.

A London physician reports from a study of 39 addicts that the death rate, from whatever cause, is about 20 times higher in heroin users than in non-users of the same ages. The specific causes of death were found to be an overdosage of heroin, withdrawal from it, infections, various kinds of accidents, and suicide.

Accidental overdosage led all other causes of death, with 12 of the 39 users dying from this cause. Suicide as a cause of death was approximately 50 times greater than is expected in an average population group and nine of the members of the group died from this cause. Even though the suicide rate in heroin users is so much greater than might be expected there is no reason to assume that the drug itself is a direct cause of suicide, but there is a possibility that new stresses and problems created by the use of heroin when superimposed on a personality that was already distressed, might well add to the likelihood of suicide over and above preexisting conditions that might predispose a person to take his own life.

Regardless of specific causes, it seems clear that the heroin addict will not live as long as a non-user on the average and the loss of years in a group of addicts will be very substantial.

blood destruction by a drug

Karpatkin, Simon. "Drug-Induced Thrombocytopenia," American Journal of the Medical Sciences, 262: 68–78, August 1971.

An Associate Professor of the New York University School of Medicine reports a case study of a patient whose blood composition was abnormal because of reaction to a drug. When the patient was taken off all drugs his blood structure slowly returned to normal.

The important part of this report resides not in the identification of a specific blood-destroying drug, but in the substantiation of the fact that almost any drug has the possibility of sensitizing someone to immunological reactions that impair or affect some part of the body. Any drug taken by a person should be under the supervision of a physician and the possibility of drug reactions must always be considered when unexpected reactions occur. Doctor Karpatkin identifies 24 other drug treatments in which blood destruction occurred and for which medical documentation was obtained.

The destruction or removal of blood platelets in the foregoing drug reactions were shown to be on a hypersensitivity or immunological basis. Immediate removal of suspected drugs resulted in complete recovery. In 14 patients whose blood platelets were being destroyed by quinidine, complete recovery was noted within three to 17 days on withdrawal of the drug. In seven patients the recovery occurred in one week, although in one person's blood serum antibodies were found for 181 days after discontinuance of the drug. Liver or kidney disease, however, may delay the recovery.

This report is concerned with the destruction of blood platelets because of a hypersensitive reaction to a drug that a patient was receiving in medical treatment under the guidance of a physician. Perhaps its primary significance lies in the fact that any drug may be hazardous and it is particularly unwise to use drugs independently of medical supervision, for their effects cannot be predicted safely by the layman and sometimes not even by the doctor. Certain it is that persons who wish to remain in good physical condition cannot afford to have an impaired blood supply due to the unwise use of drugs.

[Dr. Karpatkin's report gives added strength to the already observed fact that heroin addiction may have multiple hazards, even though the New York physician does not mention heroin. Any drug may be hazardous to a particular person irrespective of its nature because of potential individual reactions of the user. Heroin, which is injected without the medical supervision that is needed with any drug, would appear to be particularly likely to result in a failure on the part of the user to receive prompt medical care if untoward reactions occur.—Ed.]

multiple drug hazard for heroin addicts

AtLee, William E. Jr. "Talc and Cornstarch Emboli in Eyes of Drug Abusers," Journal of the American Medical Association, 219: 49–51, January 3, 1972.

A Portland eye specialist of the University of Oregon Medical School reports from studies of 17 heroin addicts and analysis of the deaths of four other heroin users, that the injection of methylphenidate hydrochloride (an amphetamine) carries the hazard of eye tissue involvement with possible impairment of vision.

The physician first became aware of this possibility when a 23-year old female heroin addict who was receiving methadone began to inject methylphenidate as well. After two months of "shooting Ritalin," as the woman explained, she began to have a reduction in her ability to see. A careful eye examination revealed tiny glistening particles that were deposited in various parts of the eye.

Severe heart and pulmonary complications that sometimes accompany the injection of Ritalin had brought the woman to the hospital and subsequent eye examination. Within one-year's time similar injections had caused the death of four addicts in the Portland area and Dr. AtLee was able to confirm at autopsy the presence of the glistening particles in the eye tissues of one of these addicts.

The physician was able to arrange careful eye examinations of other addicts in the area who were injecting methylphenidate (Ritalin). In 14 addicts without loss of vision the eye specialist was nevertheless able to detect in every one of them the glistening particles that had invaded the eye tissues. Two other addicts reported visual impairment following the use of methylphenidate. Both had also experienced acute failure of the right side of the heart and high blood pressure in the lungs.

Dr. AtLee reports that in the Portland area methylphenidate is used in the greatest quantity by heroin addicts receiving methadone maintenance. Although many of the addicts report difficult breathing at the time of injection few of the addicts are hospitalized for this form of drug abuse, according to the Portland physician.

It appears to be the talc and cornstarch filler of the methylphenidate tablet that is deposited as minute glistening crystals in the eye tissues with resultant damage to vision. The crystals have also been found by other investigators in the lungs, heart valves, liver, spleen and kidneys.

The doctor concludes that the finding of such crystals in the retina and choroid of the eye should cause the physician to suspect drug abuse on the part of the patient. Such a finding therefore becomes one more diagnostic criterion by which an addict may be identified.

kidney disease linked with heroin

Kilcoyne, Margaret, John J. Daly, David J. Gocke, Gerald E. Thomson, Jay I. Meltzer, Konrad C. Hsu and Myron Tannenbaum. "Nephrotic Syndrome in Heroin Addicts," Lancet, II (No. 7740), 17–20, January 1, 1972.

Seven medical specialists of New York City observe that symptoms of kidney disease related to heroin addiction have not been well recognized in the past. They report the finding of kidney disease in eight heroin addicts, verified by electron and special microscopic techniques and biopsies (living tissue study) from kidney tissues, as well as by clinical evidence of the disorder.

In this study the eight heroin addicts came for medical or hospital care within a period of three months. They had used heroin for two to 23 years and three of the addicts obtained their heroin from the same pusher. None had ever had kidney disease in the past.

[Extensive study revealed unusual changes in the kidneys, not ordinarily found in kidney disease. Depositions of materials, biochemical alterations, immunological changes and other shifts away from normal cannot be adequately described in a non-technical condensation such as this one. If technical information is desired, the original article should be consulted by the reader.—Ed.]

The investigators in this study were unable to identify the cause of the kidney disorder with certainty, but concluded that evidence of antibody action found in the kidney tissues makes it likely that the disorder resulted from virus or bacterial infections resulting from an injection of heroin, from toxic or injurious substances used to dilute the drug, or from the heroin itself. The possibility of an allergic reaction to heroin or the substances in which it is diluted is supported by the findings of a few others who have found evidence of an allergic or immune reaction in heroin addicts.

7

withdrawal symptoms

Whenever the heroin addict is unable to obtain his drug on schedule he may suffer mild to severe withdrawal symptoms, depending on the level of physical dependence to which he is bound. Unless the addict has some handicap such as heart disease or other medical problem, it is unlikely that withdrawal symptoms will be so severe as to threaten life. However, under certain circumstances, as with a newly born infant, the added stress may result in a fatal combination. In such an instance the recognition of withdrawal symptoms and the beginning of proper medical treatment may be lifesaving.

Formerly, no specific treatment was provided for the control of the distress of the heroin addict when he could not get his drug, but tranquilizers have been found to be useful in modern treatments and other drugs have been used by physicians with some caution. Often, the patient with mild withdrawal symptoms may need no specific medication. In the old days, in fact, the addict was expected to suffer through his withdrawal as a regular part of his treatment for addiction.

withdrawal symptoms

Trellis, Emil S. "Narcotics Use and Abuse," Pennsylvania Medicine, 69: 50-52, May 1966.

The medical director of the Narcotics Addiction Treatment Program of Western Pennsylvania observes that as increasing amounts of narcotics are used tolerance to the drugs occurs not only in the central nervous system, but in other organ systems as well.

After several weeks of increasing tolerance (with increasingly large dosages of drugs) withdrawal symptoms will appear in the addict if his narcotic is abruptly discontinued.

Withdrawal symptoms of the opiates, including heroin, include a variety of conditions, such as chills, nausea, loss of appetite, restlessness, inability to sleep, yawning, sweating, excessive production of tears, twitching of muscles, vomiting, diarrhea, and dilation of the pupils along with cramping from muscle distress.

If the patient suffering withdrawal symptoms has some other health problem such as heart disease, diabetes, or kidney disease, the added stress of the withdrawal symptoms (from heroin) may cause death. Usually, however, the pain and distress begin to subside after three or four days (and disappear within a few more days).

withdrawal symptoms in the
newborn addict

*Mims, LeRoy C. and Harris D. Riley, Jr. "The Narcotic With-
drawal Syndrome in the Newborn Infant," Journal of the
Oklahoma State Medical Association, 62: 411–412 (No. 9),
September 1969.*

Two physicians express their concern for the newborn narcotic addict in an editorial published in a state medical journal. The two doctors observe that in recent years there has
been a remarkable increase on a national scale in the use of
narcotics and the development of addiction in females of
childbearing age.

During pregnancy the unborn child becomes dependent if
the mother-to-be continues her narcotic addiction. At birth
the newborn infant is suddenly shut off from his supply of
narcotics which he has been receiving from the mother's
bloodstream. Within hours the infant will be suffering withdrawal symptoms that may threaten his life.

At the University of Oklahoma Medical Center a newly-
born infant began to develop narcotic withdrawal symptoms
within 24 hours. Physicians were able to document the fact
that the mother of the infant was addicted to morphine and
were alert to the possibility that the baby might need treatment for withdrawal symptoms.

The baby began to develop extreme irritability, suffered
from diarrhea, nausea and vomiting. The infant cried frequently, and for prolonged periods of time in a high-pitched,
shrill tone of voice. Other symptoms included yawning and

sneezing, tremors (tremblings and shakings), flushed skin, profuse sweating and fever. Sometimes profound shock, convulsions and death may occur, although in this case the baby was treated promptly because of the anticipated reactions and recovered satisfactorily.

Failure to recognize narcotic withdrawal symptoms in the newborn baby with consequent failure to render appropriate medical treatment means that approximately 95 per cent of the infants addicted to drugs at birth will die. Thus, there is an overwhelming risk of death for the baby if the condition is not recognized, say these two physicians. In one study it was found that of 37 addicted babies who were not treated, 33 died.

heroin and the newborn infant

Zelson, Carl. "Heroin Withdrawal Syndrome," The Journal of Pediatrics, 76: 483–484, March 1970.

A Professor of Pediatrics of the New York Medical College and Metropolitan Hospital reports on his experiences with and observations of 371 babies born of mothers addicted to drugs over a period of nine years.

Dr. Zelson believes that it might be advisable to treat all infants born of mothers using heroin without waiting for withdrawal symptoms to develop. Treatment is simple and harmless. As a rule the infants respond to a proper dosage of chlorpromazine within 24 hours and remain in quiet sleep from feeding to feeding, according to the New York physician. However, the doctor believes that when research is being done with babies born of mothers addicted to heroin that evidence of withdrawal symptoms on the part of the infants should be clearcut. In such studies he thinks there should be progressive evidence of the intensity of tremors and irritability, and perhaps other symptoms in order to justify the need for treatment.

At the Metropolitan Hospital approximately 50 per cent of the babies needed treatment for 10 to 21 days, but 27 per cent of them needed treatment up to 40 days.

Four per cent of the addict babies died despite medical treatment.

diabetic acidosis after withdrawal

from heroin

Desser, Kenneth B. "Diabetic Ketoacidosis During Acute Heroin Abstinence," The Lancet, 2: 689–690, September 27, 1969.

Two members of the Department of Medicine of the Beth Israel Medical Center in New York City observe that the medical complications of narcotic addiction often reveal unusual disease patterns.

The two physicians report the case of a 17-year old heroin addict who came to the hospital with complaints of abdominal pain and thirst. He had been injecting two "bags" of heroin a day for about one year. During the two months prior to hospital admission he had lost body weight and begun to urinate a great deal. Three days before coming to the hospital he decided to stop using heroin and 12 hours later became restless and sweaty, had chills, a runny nose, muscular cramps, thirst and excessive urination. His rate and depth of respiration increased and he had intense abdominal pain.

At the hospital it was found he had the heredity for diabetes mellitus. Laboratory studies revealed facts that led to the diagnosis of diabetes and he was treated accordingly and discharged one week later.

The physicians believed that the sudden withdrawal of heroin [in this single case—Ed.] contributed to the production of a profound metabolic disorder and diabetic acidosis.

multiple drug addiction increases the hazard of withdrawal from heroin

Bewley, Thomas H. and Oved Ben-Arie. "Physical Dependence on Heroin and Pentobarbitone," The Practitioner, 200: 251–253, February 1968.

Two members of the staff of the Tooting Bec Hospital in London say that when an addict is physically dependent on more than one drug at the same time withdrawal can be a complex matter. Often one drug must be withdrawn gradually even though the other is stopped at once. The physician's judgment as to which drug should be stopped may be an important decision.

The dose of heroin that a person has been taking must be accurately determined if he is to be put on methadone, which may later be gradually withdrawn if that is the treatment desired. Opiates can usually be withdrawn in 10 to 14 days with no withdrawal symptoms.

When the addict is also physically addicted to barbiturates it may be wise for the doctor to get him to the point of mild signs of intoxication from overdosage, in order to avoid certain hazardous symptoms of withdrawal (such as convulsions).

The doctors report the case of a man who was physically dependent on alcohol who terminated that dependency when he developed a tolerance for heroin. Then he became addicted to barbiturates and rapidly deteriorated in social and economic integration. At various times he had taken large doses of heroin, cocaine and pentobarbitone. The patient was finally withdrawn from opiates and barbiturates without symptoms of abstinence from either drug. The specific withdrawal methods are described by the physicians in the original article.

[English observations that multiple drug abuse by an individual is more hazardous than an addiction to a single drug is in keeping with demonstrated knowledge that drugs often interact with each other in unpredictable ways, as well as with the American evidence that drug users who multiply their addictions are less apt to be treated successfully, undoubtedly in part due to greater disturbance of personalities than is ordinarily found in other addicts.—Ed.]

withdrawal symptoms in infants

Reddy, A. Mahender, Rita G. Harper and Gertrude Stern. "Observations on Heroin and Methadone Withdrawal in the Newborn," Pediatrics, 48: 353–358, September 1971.

Three Brooklyn physicians report on their studies of 40 infants who were born to mothers addicted to heroin. All of the newly-born babies developed withdrawal symptoms within hours after their births, except for six babies who did not show any evidence of narcotic addiction. Most of the babies were below normal weight at birth and seven were premature. None of the infants had any serious congenital malformations.

Symptoms involving the brain and nervous system in general predominated in babies who showed withdrawal symptoms. The babies were hyperactive, irritable and had tremors. Later the digestive system was involved, with 44 per cent of the infants feeding poorly, regurgitating food, vomiting or having diarrhea. These symptoms usually came between the fourth and sixth day of life. Other symptoms occurred in a minority such as elevation of temperature, nasal congestion and sneezing. These symptoms occurred in about six per cent of the total group, compared to 100 per cent with nervous system symptoms and 44 per cent with digestive disorders.

The babies were treated with paregoric or phenobarbital to control their withdrawal symptoms from heroin and gradually reduced in amount unless the symptoms recurred. Treatment with phenobarbital usually lasted about 18 days and with paregoric for about 30 days.

Three babies born to mothers receiving methadone showed essentially the same withdrawal symptoms as the infants born to mothers on heroin. Treatment was also similar. Possibly the methadone mothers might have been using heroin as well and concealing the fact from the physicians. The six babies who showed no withdrawal symptoms were all born to mothers who said they used heroin only occasionally.

Previous medical investigators have reported a high incidence of congenital defects, but the heroin mothers in this study had babies without any obvious severe malformations at birth.

At birth the babies were quite free of any respiratory depression even in those cases where the mothers had taken heroin only one or two hours before birth of the baby. It might be assumed that a powerful narcotic such as heroin would have a depressant effect on the baby's breathing, but the latter, being an addict like the mother, tolerates the drug even before birth.

tranquilizer treatment of withdrawal symptoms

Mulvaney, Robert B. J. "Treatment of Narcotic Withdrawal Symptoms," Diseases of the Nervous System, 27: 329–330, January 1966.

A physician of the Essex County Penitentiary in New Jersey reports on 18 months of experience in the treatment of withdrawal symptoms among heroin addicts in prison.

At the time of admission to prison the addicts had typically been using one to three "bags" of heroin daily for about three months. When first seen by Doctor Mulvaney the prisoners had been without their narcotics for the three days consumed in their trial, conviction, and commitment procedures.

The addicts complained of being "nervous," "jumpy," "tense," or "keyed up." The doctor was usually called when the prisoners began to suffer abdominal pain, nausea, weakness, heartburn and inability to sleep.

The physician reports that the tranquilizing agent thioridazine was so successful in the control of distress that it soon superseded all other forms of treatment of the withdrawal symptoms, which usually disappeared after about seven to 10 days. Return of the ability to sleep was one of the major advantages of the treatment, according to Dr. Mulvaney.

respiration of newborn premature

infants addicted to heroin

Glass, Leonard, B. K. Rajegowda and Hugh E. Evans. "Absence of Respiratory Distress Syndrome in Premature Infants of Heroin-Addicted Mothers," Lancet, II (No. 7726), September 25, 1971.

Three physicians of Columbia University and the Harlem Hospital Center in New York City report a study of 33 premature babies who were born to mothers addicted to heroin.

The medical records of 33 premature infants who were showing heroin withdrawal symptoms at or after birth were studied in respect to the presence or absence of respiratory distress. It was found that this condition was exceedingly rare among the premature infant addicts and less than the rate of acute respiratory distress in infants who were not heroin addicts at birth.

Although the investigators had no explanation of this surprising finding [since difficulty in breathing is generally accepted as one of the signs of heroin addiction in the newborn—Ed.] they did observe that in infant addicts they had consistently found respiratory alkalosis on the first day of life and that when acute respiratory distress occurs it is associated with an acidosis. Thus, the investigators raise the question as to whether or not the alkalosis protects the premature infant addicted to heroin against the development of difficulty in breathing.

[Further research on the subject is needed since the physicians could find no specific cause for their findings. It appears from this study that babies addicted to heroin and suffering from withdrawal symptoms may not give evidence of respiratory distress and that the absence of this diagnostic feature must be taken into account for proper diagnosis and treatment of the newborn of mothers who are heroin addicts.—Ed.]

8

sudden death from the injection of heroin

Although the medical profession does not have complete knowledge of the cause of death in all cases of heroin injection, it does have enough information to verify that fatal reactions have occurred because of the drug. A presumptive diagnosis of death from intravenous narcoticism, as a matter of fact, may be made at the scene of the initial finding of the body in about 85 per cent of the cases, with confirmation by autopsy, chemical, and microscopic techniques. [One authority reports that New York City medical examiners, on the other hand, often do *not* find chemical evidence of opiates. There must be additional means of determining cause of death.—Ed.] The depression of respiration, the swelling of lung tissue, anaphylactic shock due to contaminating substances in the heroin mixture, and inability to anticipate the strength of the injected heroin are some of the reasons why addicts die from the use of heroin. Complications of infections, blood clots, and other conditions that may cause impairment of health and death are discussed primarily in the chapter on the effects associated with the use of heroin. This chapter is more concerned with the sudden death of addicts that appear to be immediately related to injection of the drug.

basis for diagnosis of death from injection of a drug

Siegel, Henry, Milton Helpern and Theodore Ehrenreich. "The Diagnosis of Death from Intravenous Narcotism," Journal of Forensic Sciences, 11: 1–16, January 1966.

Three physicians from the Office of the Chief Medical Examiner in New York City discuss the criteria that are used in concluding that a person had died from an injection of a narcotic drug. Autopsy findings and the results of microscopic study of body tissues are emphasized in the report.

One hundred consecutive deaths from the injection of drugs, primarily of heroin, were studied and found to be typical of similar findings encountered by the physicians over a number of years with a much larger number of addicts whose deaths were related to the injection of narcotic substances.

At the scene of the death it was possible to make a presumptive diagnosis of a fatal reaction to drugs in 85 per cent of the cases. Only in 15 per cent of the deaths was heroin not suspected at first. The presumptive diagnosis was based on finding the body in a certain place such as a roof, hallway, lavatory, or locked hotel room, the observation of froth in the mouth and nose, fresh needle puncture, or scarred vein.

Various tissues and fluids of the body were analyzed. Opiates were found by chemical means in tissues in 30 per cent of the dead addicts. Sometimes death had occurred so rapidly that the injection was not completed and no opiates were detected in the body. [In such cases death may be caused by arrythmia or anaphylaxis.—Ed.]

Autopsy and microscopic findings were the most conclusive factors in diagnosis of death from injection of a drug. Four major parts of the body provided useful information: the injection site, the lungs, the lymph nodes and the liver. At the injection site the examiners found fresh needle punctures, hemorrhages, and scarring. In the lungs congestion, swelling of tissues and aspirated materials were often found early and diffuse pneumonia detected later. The lymph nodes were enlarged, and the liver showed microscopic infiltration of the cells of the portal (entrance) area.

The enlargement of lymph nodes occurred primarily in the arm draining the area of injection, thus was on one side only unless both arms had been used. Lymph nodes of the liver, bile duct, and pancreas were enlarged in about 75 per cent of the cases, and were sometimes five times the normal size.

Police and medical evidence, followed by autopsy, gives sufficient basis for the diagnosis of death from the intravenous injection of a drug, according to these physicians.

deaths from heroin in new york city

Helpern, Milton and Yong-Myun Rho. "Deaths from Narcotism in New York City," New York State Journal of Medicine, 66: 2391–2408, September 15, 1966.

Two New York City physicians maintain that there is no accurate figure on the incidence of narcotic addiction today, but that there is ample evidence that the problem is increasing.

An important indicator of the extent of addiction is the number of deaths occurring from the use of heroin. Of 1,586 deaths from narcotics in New York City over a 12-year period the number of fatalities rose from 57 in 1950 to 311 in 1961. The number of deaths has continued to rise since the latter date. Approximately 59 per cent of the deaths occurred in unmarried persons and 60 per cent of the deaths were in the age group under 30 years. [By 1971 these figures had almost tripled.—Ed.]

Deaths occurred on floors, hallways, stairways, roofs, automobiles, vacant lots, streets, hospitals, bathtubs and toilet rooms and other places, even in an elevator. Sometimes bodies were not found until putrefaction had set in. Often the equipment needed for the injection of heroin was found alongside the dead body. In some cases death had occurred so rapidly that the tourniquet was still in place on the arm and the needle of the syringe was still in the skin. Sometimes the syringe was mixed with blood of the victim and residual heroin mixture. In more than one-half of the deaths the bodies of the victims were found in some other place than the place in which they lived.

Autopsy usually reveals a generalized congestion of body organs, especially in the lungs, in cases of sudden deaths of addicts. Milk is sometimes found aspirated into the lungs and seems to reflect the belief among addicts that in some way it is an antidote to an overdose of heroin. Swelling of lymph nodes in the abdomen and arm pits is also commonly found at autopsy.

900 deaths in new york city from drugs in 1969

Abelson, Philip H. "Death from Heroin," Science, 168: 1289, June 12, 1971.

The editor of *Science* comments editorially on reports of sudden deaths from heroin. More than 900 fatalities from drugs occurred in New York City alone during 1969. The majority of deaths are due to a mixture of heroin and other substances that were injected into a blood vessel.

The exact mechanism of death is not always known. Sometimes an overdosage of heroin is blamed. At other times an allergy seems to be involved. Heroin is adulterated with various additives that may contain antigens for particular addicts. Many purchases of heroin expose the user to variable amounts of the drug and an addict accustomed to low dosage may die from an injection of almost pure heroin.

It is now estimated that 200,000 persons in the United States are heroin addicts, with 100,000 in New York City alone, and it is calculated that the cost of the substance has risen to about five billion dollars annually.

deaths of young addicts

Mason, Percy. "Mortality Among Young Narcotic Addicts," Mount Sinai Hospital Journal, 34: 4-10, January-February 1967.

A physician of the Mount Sinai Hospital in New York City says that almost every doctor now comes into contact with problems of addiction. He estimates that about one per cent of the total addict population dies each year from an overdosage of drugs.

Back in 1953 in New York City there were 541 deaths due to alcoholism and 100 due to drug addiction. In terms of the alcoholic and drug addict populations of the city at that time the death rate for alcoholics was approximately 1.5 per 1,000 alcoholics and five per 1,000 addicts. Thus, the death rate for narcotic addicts was approximately three times as great as that for alcoholics.

Since the preceding date many other studies show that the narcotic addict has a very high death rate.

In this study narcotic addicts between the ages of 15 and 21 years who were admitted to the Riverside Hospital in New York City because of heroin usage revealed that of 66 deaths of male addicts 39 were from an overdosage of the drug. Although one-third of the patients used barbiturates, not one death was recorded from this kind of drug.

A strong proportion of these fatal cases involved mental illness. Approximately two-thirds of the addicts who died had personality disorders, one-fourth had schizophrenia and a small minority had psychoneurosis.

After treatment at the hospital approximately 19 per cent died within seven days after discharge, 30 per cent in less than a month, 49 per cent within three months and 70 per cent in less than one year.

heroin deaths in england

Bewley, Thomas H., Oved Ben-Arie and I. Pierce James. "Morbidity and Mortality from Heroin Dependence 1: Survey of Heroin Addicts Known to Home Office," British Medical Journal, 1: 725-726, March 23, 1968.

Three English experts on narcotic addiction report that heroin addiction in Great Britain now carries a high mortality risk. More deaths are now occurring from the use of this drug and in younger persons. New cases of opiate addiction have been doubling every 16 months.

A study of 69 deaths of heroin addicts in Great Britain showed that 23 per cent had committed suicide, 29 per cent had died from an overdosage of the drug, and 48 per cent had died from violence, infection, or other causes.

The death rate in non-therapeutic heroin addicts (those not receiving the drug from physicians for treatment of their addiction) was 28 times the expected rate. Of the deaths 40 per cent involved addicts under the age of 20 years.

death of heroin addict after return to
his usual dose of the drug

Todd, J. "Decreased Tolerance to Heroin," British Medical Journal, 2: 120-121, April 13, 1968.

An English physician comments that one cause of death of heroin addicts after a period of withdrawal from the drug is the decrease of tolerance that follows a period of hospitalization or imprisonment during which time no access to the drug has been achieved.

When the addict gets out of the hopsital or prison and again has access to his drug he is apt to begin again with the previous dosage to which he was accustomed. Because of his decrease in tolerance for heroin he suffers from an overdose.

This fatal miscalculation resulted in the death of a heroin addict known to the English doctor and he believes that greater attention to this hazard should be given by physicians and others.

blue velvet and the death of addicts

Burton, John F., Edward S. Zawadzki, Herbert R. Wetherell and Thomas W. Moy. "Mainliners and Blue Velvet," Journal of Forensic Sciences, 10: 466-472, October 1965.

Two physicians and two associates from Detroit reported in 1965 that a sharp rise had occurred in sudden deaths associated with the injection of various drugs. About three persons were dying each month from drug reactions in patients who came to the doctors' offices. A combination of drugs called "blue velvet" was found to be responsible for many of the deaths. The mixture involved an antihistamine and a narcotic.

A case history involves a 25-year old male who collapsed while visiting friends. He was rushed to a nearby hospital where he was dead on arrival. Autopsy revealed needle marks and keloid scars over various blood vessels. The heart was enlarged and distended with blood. The lungs were heavy and wet. The respiratory channels were filled with white foam and watery fluid. The urine contained an alkaloid that was identified as morphine.

Swelling of lung tissues was the paramount finding. Talc and starch were identified in the lung tissues. The talc was found to be derived from the antihistamine. Evidence was found at autopsy of repeated showers of small blood clots that lodged in the lungs without fatal results. Sudden death was judged by the physicians as being due to enlargement of the right ventricle of the heart because of increased resistance of the lungs to blood pumped to them by this part of the heart. Thus, death was judged to be the result of repeated injections of "blue velvet" with massive swelling of lung tissue and enlargement of the heart

near death from respiratory failure

Werner, Arnold. "Near-Fatal Hyperacute Reaction to Intra- venously Administered Heroin," Journal of the American Medical Association, 207: 2277–2278, March 24, 1969.

A Philadelphia physician reports the case of a heroin addict who gave himself an injection of the drug in the men's room of a service station with nearly fatal results. The addict came out to drive away in his car and then slumped over its wheel as he drove out of the station.

A slight accident occurred when the stuporous addict ran into the doctor's car, but the traffic mishap probably saved the former's life as it focused the attention of the physician on the victim and he realized the man was in need of medical aid.

The physician came to the rescue of the addict immediately. He applied mouth-to-mouth breathing and external cardiac massage when he found that the man had no respiration, no pulse, and no heart sounds.

The victim began to recover by the time the ambulance and police arrived. He was then sitting up and was able to answer questions. Later he admitted that he had given himself an injection of heroin.

Dr. Werner concluded that the man's near-fatal experience was due to the effect of heroin on the respiratory center of the brain and that the victim would have died if he had not been given mouth-to-mouth resuscitation without delay.

9

multiple drug usage by heroin addicts

The heroin addict has usually exposed himself to a multiplicity of drugs and almost invariably turns to another drug when he cannot obtain his normal supplies of the former. The use of barbiturates, cocaine, sedatives, tranquilizers and other drugs, including marijuana, is commonplace and has usually preceded heroin, but may also be taken in conjunction with the latter or in lieu of it. The widespread use of multiple drugs by the heroin addict adds to the hazards of his affliction for complicated mechanisms and can increase the occurrence and severity of reactions that are not expected.

stepping stones to heroin addiction

Weppner, Robert S. and Michael H. Agar. "Immediate Precursors to Heroin Addiction," Journal of Health and Social Behavior, 12: 10-18, March 1971.

Two investigators of the National Institute and Mental Health Clinical Research Center in Lexington observe that any drug use at any time in an addict's life could be interpreted as a stepping stone to heroin. Many recent studies have explored the possibility that marijuana may be a precursor to the use of heroin. The results of these studies are in conflict.

The investigators thought that there may be many drugs that may lead to heroin addiction and that these drugs will differ in kind in different social groupings.

In this study it was found that of 738 persons who were hooked on heroin at any time approximately 40 per cent had never been addicted to any other drug. In this group there appeared to be no immediate precursor to heroin addiction.

In the study group 446 of the heroin addicts had been previously addicted to some other drug. Of these heroin addicts approximately 36 per cent had used marijuana as a precursor to heroin. Alcohol ranked second as a preceding drug with approximately 18 per cent being hooked on this substance before turning to heroin. Other narcotics also accounted for approximately 18 per cent as a precursor to heroin. Thus, among the group in approximately 36 per cent of the cases marijuana was the preceding drug whereas in the remaining two-thirds majority various other substances were involved. Marijuana and alcohol appear to be the most common substances on which persons are hooked before they become addicted to heroin.

The investigators found that heroin users abused a wide range of drugs immediately before heroin.

The three independent drugs most frequently abused prior to heroin addiction are marijuana, alcohol and cough syrup. The investigators observed that marijuana is illegal, cough syrup is easily obtainable in most states and alcohol is legal. Few investigators have considered alcoholism as an important stepping stone to heroin addiction. [The two research workers appear to verify in this study that there is no single drug that can be described as a definite precursor to the heroin habit.—Ed.]

mechanisms of drug interactions

Solomon, Harvey M., Marian J. Barakat and Constance J. Ashley. "Mechanisms of Drug Interaction," Journal of the American Medical Association, 216: 1997–1999, June 21, 1971.

A physician and two associates report that one drug may change the actions of another drug in the human body in many different ways.

One drug may change the rate at which another is metabolized in the body; it may alter the rate at which a drug is excreted, the degree of absorption from the gastrointestinal tract; it may displace another drug chemically from the place where it is bound to protein.

New interactions between multiple drugs in the body are continually being reported by physicians and research workers from clinical and laboratory evidence. The metabolism (chemical disposition within the body) of drugs is dependent upon enzymes of the liver that make the drugs less toxic and more easily excreted from the body in one form or another.

Although this report is mostly concerned with the effects of multiple drugs on the clotting process, the significance for drugs in general is extensive. The drug addict who takes multiple drugs cannot predict with certainty how the actions of one may affect those of another. Some of the effects are hazardous to life and health even when they are not fully understood. Although this report is perhaps too technical for the layman reader its implication is not. Multiple drug usage can be a dangerous procedure.

heroin, barbiturates, and other drugs

Mitcheson, Martin, David Hawks, James Davidson, Laura Hitchens and Sarah Malone. "Sedative Abuse by Heroin Addicts," The Lancet, 1: 606–607, March 21, 1970.

Five members of the staff of the Addiction Research Unit of the Institute of Psychiatry in London indicate that heroin dependency is usually only a part of multiple drug abuse.

In the past the commonest drugs associated with heroin in England were cocaine, cannabis and the amphetamines. However, by 1967 it was found that 66 per cent of the heroin users in a London prison also took barbiturates and in 1968 sedative abuse was reported in 53 per cent of a group that was injecting amphetamines.

In this study 65 heroin addicts were interviewed in respect to their consumption of other drugs. At one time or another all of the addicts had used alcohol, marijuana and methadone. All but one of the heroin users had taken amphetamines. Sixty-two of the 65 addicts had used barbiturates and 50 of the 65 had taken cocaine (77 per cent).

In the last month prior to this study, on a daily basis, 66 per cent had been using heroin, 65 per cent methadone, 37 per cent barbiturates, 19 per cent amphetamines, 12 per cent marijuana, nine per cent cocaine and three per cent alcohol. Thus, a substantial percentage of the heroin addicts were using multiple drugs on a daily basis.

It was discovered by the research workers that 80 per cent of the heroin addicts had injected [or ingested—Ed.] barbiturates and in the case of 14 addicts this injection occurred the first time they obtained the sedatives, which came predominantly from the illicit market. Forty-two of the addicts admitted they took barbiturates "for kicks."

reactions from combinations of
heroin and barbiturates

Cumberlidge, Malcolm C. "The Abuse of Barbiturates by Heroin Addicts," Canadian Medical Association Journal, 98: 1045–1049, June 1, 1968.

A staff member of the Narcotic Addiction Foundation of British Columbia reports a study of the abuse of barbiturates by 30 heroin addicts (16 males and 14 females). The primary reason given by the addicts for combining the two drugs was the belief that the effects of heroin would be increased, although nearly as many of the drug users professed the use of barbiturates in an effort to achieve heavy sedation. However, nearly one-half said they used barbiturates because they had no heroin at the time.

Eighty-seven per cent of the addicts said they had suffered many times from acute intoxication while they were on barbiturates, either alone or with heroin, but not a single addict admitted the same results when they were on heroin alone. The primary effects of the barbiturates when consumed by the heroin addicts, in the order of greatest to least frequency, were as follows: 1) acute intoxication, with "goofy" feelings; 2) loss of consciousness; 3) memory loss; 4) lack of attention to cleanliness, clothing and nutrition; 5) feelings of degradation, and 6) withdrawal symptoms.

Loss of consciousness had occurred in 75 per cent of the males and 71 per cent of the females.

Feelings of degradation occurred because in the heroin addict subculture the use of barbiturates suggests that there has been a loss of prowess for obtaining heroin and the excitement of avoiding detection by the police has been given up.

Acute barbiturate poisoning may be accidentally or willfully superimposed upon chronic effects at any time, so that barbiturate abuse is markedly more dangerous than heroin addiction alone, since the lethal dose of the drug is not much greater in addicts than in normal persons. Barbiturates are high on the suicide list.

Withdrawal from barbiturates may be more dangerous than withdrawal from heroin and special medical, nursing, and other care may be needed to guard against delirium, convulsions, and death.

One-half of the addicts had withdrawn simultaneously from the use of both heroin and barbiturates, but 26 per cent of those who completed withdrawal returned to heroin within 24 hours, and most of the remaining addicts returned to use of the drug within a few weeks. Without exception they also returned to barbiturates whenever they could not get heroin.

interactions of drugs

Owen, John A., Jr. "Drug Interactions," Virginia Medical Monthly, 96: 35–37 (No. 1), January 1969.

An Associate Professor of Medicine of the University of Virginia School of Medicine reports that the metabolic history of any drug that is taken into the body depends upon five major steps, as follows: 1) absorption; 2) reversible binding to plasma (fluid part of the blood) or storage tissue parts; 3) action at the receptor site of the drug; 4) biotransformation (the change of drugs produced by enzymes or other products in the living body), and 5) excretion of the drug.

When two drugs are taken at the same time each may influence the behavior of the other at any one or more of the foregoing five steps. Thus, a great number of drug interactions may take place. Every new drug that is discovered may have a potential for reacting with every drug already known to medicine, and most of these potential reactions will produce more problems than benefits, according to Dr. Owen.

The ways in which drugs can complicate medical practice and the lives of individuals may be seen in the following examples.

> Tetracycline (an antibiotic) interferes with the action of penicillin (an antibiotic), so that the death rate in pneumococcal meningitis (inflammation of the brain with a certain type of germ) is higher when the patient is treated with both of these drugs than if he is treated with either one alone.

> Patients in a depression who receive treatment with a particular monoamine oxidase drug, and who then eat cheese, may suffer from a critical crisis of high blood pressure that may cause death. The component of cheese that is involved in this reaction is tyramine. The tyramine of cheese leads to certain changes in autonomic nerve endings (through the displacement of norepinephrine from the storage granules in autonomic nerve endings) which in the presence of monoamine

oxidase, diffuses out of the nerve fiber to produce intense constriction of blood vessels and high blood pressure. (Either substance taken alone is safe.)

When people who have the risk of blood clots are given Dicoumarol to prevent clotting of the blood they must be careful about taking phenobarbital. The latter drug affects the liver enzymes that act on Dicoumarol, so that larger doses of the latter drug must be given in order to prevent blood clots. More serious is the possibility that spontaneous internal bleeding may occur if the phenobarbital is stopped.

[Although the foregoing drugs do not involve heroin, the basic concept of interactions between drugs in unpredictable ways supports the implication that heroin users who use a variety of other drugs are likely to compound their reactions.—Ed.]

drug combinations

McMahon, F. Gilbert. "Drug Combinations," Journal of the American Medical Association, 216: 1008–1010, May 10, 1971.

A physician of the Tulane University School of Medicine comments on the new Food and Drug Administration policy regarding fixed drug combinations. The new policy was expressed in the *Federal Register* of February 18, 1971.

Although both the new policy of the FDA and the comments by Doctor McMahon apply to over-the-counter and prescription drugs rather than to combinations of illicit drugs secured by drug addicts, some of the observations should serve to give better understandings of the problems associated with the use of multiple drugs.

Under the new policy of the FDA, medicine that contains combinations will be removed from the market unless each active ingredient can be shown to enhance its effectiveness or to reduce the side effects of the other drug or drugs.

There are many rational combinations of drugs, according to the Tulane physician. An example is a medicine used to control diarrhea that contains a narcotic as the basic ingredient as well as a small amount of another drug so that unpleasant effects would be produced if attempts to abuse the drug were made. Thus, the patient is discouraged from becoming addicted to the medicine.

Almost all over-the-counter drugs are combinations. If such medicines contain unsafe drugs or irrational combinations they should be removed from the market. Most are relatively harmless, according to Dr. McMahon.

Of the 200 most frequently prescribed drugs in 1970 physicians included 78 with fixed drug combinations, a ratio of two in every five prescriptions. When queried 90 per cent of the responding physicians expressed the view that the combinations were desirable.

The drug addict cannot be expected to know as much as the medical profession and the Food and Drug Administration regarding the hazards of multiple drug use and it is likely that such knowledge would make little difference to the addicted person who is controlled by other motivations than his own welfare and safety. For general drug abuse education, however, it should be helpful to recognize that the undesirability of drug combinations is recognized and condemned by professional groups unless advantages can be proven.

heroin-cocaine addicts

Glatt, M. M. "Reflections on Heroin and Cocaine Addiction," The Lancet, 2: 171-172, July 24, 1965.

An English physician and consulting psychiatrist reports on the treatment of 30 narcotic addicts over a period of about two years. Almost all had been introduced to the intravenous injection of a mixture of heroin and cocaine at parties or clubs. Prior to use of this mixture almost all had used amphetamines (usually "purple hearts") and marijuana.

The patients were treated in the hospital to achieve withdrawal and were then given long-term followup treatment. Vocational training is important. The patients need supervision and encouragement in making new friends after they leave the hospital. In this report Dr. Glatt indicates that group psychotherapy gave disappointing results.

The physician reaches the conclusion that relapse of the heroin-cocaine addict is made more probable because the recognized addict can lawfully obtain drugs from a doctor more easily. [This observation was true of single drugs, not combinations, in England at the time of the report.—Ed.]

A follow-up study of the 30 patients (who had been treated in the hospital for a few weeks to as long as five months) brought discouraging results. About one-half of the ct .

addicts would not bother to give information. Only one patient had abstained from drugs, but he was working, had married, acquired a new circle of friends and came back for regular visits to the hospital. Most of the patients were still using drugs, one had entered a convent, one was in prison for forging prescriptions, and most were still unsettled.

[Dr. Glatt has had a broad experience with heroin and other narcotic addicts over a number of years and it must not be assumed that his experience is limited to two years of study, although it ought to be obvious that any physician who conducts a two-year followup investigation of 30 addicts is bound to arrive at some conclusions that merit respect.—Ed.]

spread of heroin and cocaine habit
in england

Glatt, M. M. "Heroin and Cocaine Addiction," The Lancet, 1: 910–911, April 24, 1965.

A staff member of St. Bernard's Hospital in Southall, Middlesex, England confirms from his own experience in treatment of heroin and cocaine addicts that spread of the habit takes place from user to user.

The average addict, he found, had been introduced to the drugs by a friend, an acquaintance, or a club of addicts where someone had succeeded in acquiring a surplus of drugs from a doctor, who under English law could prescribe heroin or cocaine to meet the needs of an addict.* Once a surplus has been

*At the time of this report.

obtained many of the addicts sell it. It is very difficult for a busy physician to determine exactly how much of a drug the addict needs; thus the latter may get more than he needs. Then, in particular, he becomes a source for spreading narcotic addiction.

follow-up study of heroin and

cocaine addicts

Bewley, Thomas. "Heroin and Cocaine Addiction," The Lancet, 1: 808–810, April 10, 1965.

A London psychiatrist reported in 1965 that a small epidemic of addiction to heroin and cocaine had developed in the English city by means of spreading from addict to addict. The known users of heroin and cocaine amounted to only 12 in the year 1958, but this figure had grown steadily to 166 in 1963.

In this study the author reports a follow-up investigation of 33 users of heroin and cocaine over a period of two years. The 33 users of this combination of narcotic drugs had a record of being admitted to Dr. Bewley's hospital 50 times during the two-year period. In addition, the same 33 combination drug users were admitted to other mental hospitals for a total of 33 times. Hospital admissions ranged from zero to six for different addicts.

Over a period of two years the addicts had a total of 83 hospital admissions. Eleven of the addicts had died from overdosages of barbiturates, other drugs, and massive blood infections. One addict was still in the hospital and three were being detained in a mental hospital. Four addicts were deported back to Canada and the United States. One had brain surgery. Another addict was imprisoned for 12 months after leaving the hospital. One had returned to school and one had been off drugs for 10 months at the time of this report.

[The high prevalence of hospital admissions of drug abusers and the social and legal complications of their addiction, the high number of deaths from overdosage and the small number of cures emphasizes that the English experience with heroin is comparable to that of the United States.—Ed.]

signs of barbiturate dependence
on withdrawal

Hamburger, Ernest. "Barbiturate Use in Narcotic Addicts," Journal of the American Medical Association, 189: 366–368, August 3, 1964.

A physician of Lexington, Kentucky U.S. Public Health Service Hospital reported a study of 1,000 narcotic addicts in order to determine the frequency with which barbiturates are used in conjunction with another drug. Of 732 heroin addicts in the group, it was found that 228 did use barbiturates. Signs of physical dependence on barbiturates were observed in approximately 23 per cent of the 1,000 addicts. Nearly 10 per cent more claimed to be dependent on barbiturates although there was no physical evidence of such dependency.

Clinical evidence of dependence on barbiturates may appear whenever the addict takes an amount of the drug beyond his tolerance. Acute intoxication develops with signs and symptoms such as the following: difficulty in concentration, mood shifts, irritability, self-neglect, infantile behavior, rapid movement of the eyes from side to side, speech disturbance, lack of muscular coordination on standing, and longer periods of sleep.

Withdrawal signs and symptoms occur in the addict if he must abstain from barbiturates. Generally the symptoms appear in the following order, though not necessarily so: restlessness and anxiety, irritability, inability to sleep, a rise in body temperature up to about 105 degrees Fahrenheit in the late stages, rapid pulse increase of 16 to 36 beats per minute on rising from a lying down or sitting position, low blood pressure and increasing muscle tone. Delirium and convulsions may follow, and if relief is not given with barbiturates or a substitute drug, coma and death may follow.

Thus, if the addict becomes dependent on barbiturates, he gives physical signs of his addiction during intoxication. If he is withdrawn from barbiturates he reveals his addiction with different signs and symptoms. In either case, the alert physician can make a diagnosis of barbiturate dependence and can take appropriate measures.

paregoric and other drug mixtures

Lerner, A. Martin and Frederick J. Oerther. "Characteristics and Sequelae of Paregoric Abuse," Annals of Internal Medicine, 65: 1019–1030, November 1966.

Two physicians of the Wayne State University School of Medicine in Detroit report that arrests for paregoric addiction in that city exceeded those for heroin usage over a three-year period of 1962 to 1964.

In the early 18th Century paregoric was a complex mixture of drugs containing opium. Modern paregoric contains morphine along with benzoic acid, camphor, and anise oil. These latter substances have limited solubilities, are irritants, and can lead to the rapid hardening and closing of blood vessels into which they may be injected. As a consequence, larger veins are sought by paregoric users. A scar in the vicinity of the jugular vein is highly suggestive of paregoric addiction, because this vein is both large and readily accessible for the addict.

Often paregoric is mixed with other drugs, including amphetamines, barbiturates or tripelennamine tablets before injection.

At the Detroit Receiving Hospital 257 paregoric addicts were admitted during a nine-months period, mostly with symptoms of drug withdrawal, but one in seven was admitted because of a serious infection. Thirty-three of the patients had probable bacterial infections; eight had virus infections of the liver. Pus-forming infections and abscesses were common. One patient had a brain abscess and another had a pus-containing inflammation of the lining of the brain (meningitis). Seven patients had infections of the heart and five died. A variety of other health problems were found in the paregoric addicts, including difficult breathing and chest discomfort, inflammation of blood vessels and so on. Several of the patients were autopsied after death and the small pulmonary arteries of the lungs were found to be blocked by blood clots, starch granules and talc crystals, which are commonly found in heroin mixtures.

Paregoric addiction has declined dramatically in Detroit since the drug can now be obtained only by medical prescription.

ninety per cent failure of gradual withdrawal treatment of heroin addicts on multiple drugs

Hicks, Robert Carey. "The Management of Heroin Addiction at a General Hospital Drug Addiction Treatment Centre," British Journal of Addiction, 64: 235–243, October 1969.

An English physician of the Royal Infirmary of Edinburgh reports a study of the treatment of 57 heroin addicts who used multiple drugs and who came to a drug addiction treatment center of a general hospital on an out-patient basis.

Ninety-six per cent of the heroin addicts in this study had abused other drugs before beginning the use of heroin. Of 49 addicts who identified these drugs the percentage of users was as follows: amphetamines by mouth 82, cannabis (marijuana) 76, methyl-amphetamine by injection 24, cocaine by injection 20, LSD 16, morphine 12, barbiturates 10, methadone six, a variety of other drugs 10.

Previous treatment for drug addiction for 61 per cent had been provided by private physicians, for 41 per cent in psychiatric hospitals, for 18 per cent in general hospitals and for 12 per cent by general practitioners. Since all of the patients were again seeking treatment for heroin addiction it is obvious that all previous treatments had failed.

In this study the gradual withdrawal of drugs was attempted on an out-patient basis. Over a period of from one to 19 weeks of treatment only five of the addicts were withdrawn from heroin, a failure rate of approximately 90 per cent.

In conclusion Dr. Hicks admits that the treatment of heroin addiction in out-patient clinics is a notable failure. [This conclusion may or may not be supported by similar experiments in the United States.—Ed.]

10

treatments without methadone

Medical and psychiatric authorities have had a long and unrewarding experience in the treatment of narcotic addicts. Abrupt or gradual withdrawal from the opiates, under medical supervision for the treatment of complications, is a method of treatment long used in the United States with short-term success and long-range failure. Supplemented with psychiatric services this form of treatment has sometimes produced better results, but in general they have been unsatisfactory. Newer methods such as those in Synanon have emerged for treatment of narcotic addiction and large claims of success have been made, but objective and scientific research to verify such pretensions are strangely missing from the medical and scientific literature; so that one is left with doubts and misgivings about these procedures.

Some scientists and medical personnel have been so discouraged that they have raised the question as to whether or not the narcotic addict can ever be truly cured. A variety of narcotic antagonists are now available for the treatment and prevention of drug addiction and may prove to be the most satisfactory treatment of the future, but this possibility remains to be seen. The use of methadone for the control of many problems associated with heroin addiction is discussed in the next chapter.

kinds of treatment services for addicts
in the united states

Winick, Charles and Herbert Bynder. "Facilities for Treatment and Rehabilitation of Narcotic Drug Users and Addicts," American Journal of Public Health, 57: 1025–1033, June 1967.

Two consultants of the American Social Health Association made a survey of 165 facilities in the United States for treatment of the drug addict. The study also revealed the kinds of services, or treatments provided in these facilities.

The kinds of treatment for drug addicts being provided in the United States by these 165 facilities were as follows. Group or individual psychotherapy was being provided by 22 per cent of these facilities. Medical treatment, including detoxification and withdrawal, were also provided by 22 per cent of the facilities. Fourteen per cent provided guidance and casework services, 13 per cent rendered vocational and recreational therapy, 11 per cent made referrals to other agencies for needed help, seven per cent attempted treatment and rehabilitation efforts of an unspecified type and nine per cent engaged in other services. In two per cent of the facilities no direct aid was given.

No indication was given in this study of the effectiveness of the different kinds of treatment provided by the facilities, but for a more extended analysis of the facilities themselves the original report should be consulted.

the handling of drug reactions

Holcenberg, John S. and Lawrence M. Halpern. "Drug Therapy: II Treatment of Drug Misuse," Northwest Medicine, 69: 31–33 (No. 1), January 1970.

Because heroin addicts frequently use multiple drugs their needs for medical treatment may be complicated by the latter, so that it becomes essential for the physician and others to have some understanding of the diverse kinds of emergency problems that may be associated with heroin abuse.

A physician and a pharmacologist of the University of Washington School of Medicine in Seattle discuss the treatment of various categories of drug reactions.

Solvent inhalation. Harmful effects of vapor sniffing differ according to the substance that is inhaled, but the greatest danger appears to be suffocation in a plastic bag. Emergency care of acute, severe intoxication requires the establishment of adequate ventilation (artificial respiration) and observation for toxic side effects.

Stimulant drugs. Overdosage with amphetamines is apt to cause disorganized behavior, inability to sleep, paranoid ideas which may lead to violent acts, hallucinations and other symptoms. Withdrawal may present a serious psychiatric problem with depression, fatigue, sleepiness and hunger for about a week. Patients must be watched for suicide attempts. Sedatives, tranquilizers, or mood elevators should be avoided, as little is known about possible drug reactions in overdosage with amphetamines.

Sedatives, hypnotics and minor tranquilizers. These drugs may accentuate the depressant effects of each other and the latter may be further emphasized if alcohol, antihistamines, or phenothiazines are taken. These drugs are hazardous because they may alter the metabolism of other drugs as well as having their own depressant effects. Proper care calls for hospitalization in an intensive care unit that gives support to respiration, treatment of shock and the use of antibiotics to prevent pneumonia. Barbiturate overdosage, followed by removal from the drug, may lead to convulsions, which should be prevented in a hospital with declining dosages of the drug.

Hallucinogenic drugs. Bad trips are relatively low in occurrence and are best treated by a sympathetic, calm person who gives reassurance. Rarely is any drug treatment needed.

Narcotics. Nalorphine (Nalline) can be used to counter respiratory depression caused by the opiate drugs, but it has a relatively short duration of action and must be given repeatedly. Nalorphine must be used with extreme caution by the physician since it may cause an exaggerated withdrawal reaction with convulsions. Otherwise, treatment is much the same as with the sedatives (see above) with declining dosages of the drug to which the patient is addicted.

Marijuana. Infrequently, marijuana users may show stomach upsets, paranoid agitation and hysterical rigidity of several hours duration, according to the authors. Reassurance and bed rest seem adequate. The long-term effects of marijuana are not known.

drug overdosage

Cherubin, Charles E. "Acute Addictive States," New York State Journal of Medicine, 71: 2391-2394, October 15, 1971.

A physician of the Metropolitan Hospital and New York Medical College reports that more and more drug abusers are being seen in hospital emergency rooms and often constitute problems in diagnosis and treatment. That part of the report that deals with heroin follows.

An overdose of opiates such as morphine, codeine, heroin, Dilaudid or Demerol causes a somnolent or stuporous condition and in larger doses, a profound coma. Respiration is slow, the face may be bluish in color and the pupils pinpoint in size. Thus three major symptoms suggest narcotic overdosage: coma, slow breathing and constricted pupils.

Dr. Cherubin's article is much more comprehensive than the foregoing paragraph as it covers signs and symptoms of overdosage of the major categories of drugs, both in respect to overdosage and treatment. His report should be studied in full for an exposition of the diagnosis and treatment of these other drugs.

failure of psychotherapy and withdrawl

LaRouche, Maurice L. and Patrick T. Donlon. "Heroin Addiction: A Comparison of Two Inpatient Treatment Methods," Michigan Medicine, 69: 751-754, September 1970.

Two Detroit physicians report a study of 10 heroin addicts who were withdrawn from the drug while in the hospital as compared to 10 heroin addicts who were given methadone while in the hospital.

The withdrawal method without methadone resulted in unsatisfactory results. Three of the addicts signed themselves out of the hospital without medical approval, all were irritable and uncooperative or lukewarm in psychotherapeutic procedures. Many became demanding and manipulative and brought out negative attitudes on the part of the hospital staff. One addict entered jail at the time of hospital discharge and the results of psychotherapy were unsatisfactory. All 10 heroin addicts went back to the use of the drug.

Withdrawal with methadone gave better results. Of the 10 heroin users three returned to previous drug patterns and were released from the study. The remaining seven addicts have experimented with heroin infrequently and showed ability to hold a job, avoid police arrests and improve family relationships.

The two physicians observe that unfortunately psychiatric treatment of the heroin addict has never been completely satisfactory and that in this study, despite psychiatric treatment in the hospital and offer of psychiatric help after discharge from the hospital, all 10 heroin addicts who did not receive methadone relapsed back to heroin.

treatment of addicts with maintenance
dosage, psychotherapy and withdrawal

Frankau, Lady. "Treatment in England of Canadian Patients Addicted to Narcotic Drugs," Canadian Medical Association Journal, 90: 421-424, February 8, 1964.

A London physician says people addicted to drugs are sick people and that nearly all of them suffer from psychoneurosis or have a psychopathic personality.

Personality disorders precede addiction. According to Dr. Frankau, addicted persons are antisocial, inadequate, immature, unstable, selfish and self-centered and without interest in others, being solely concerned with their own problems.

"They have failed to develop normal human relationships and are almost totally without concern for the distress they inflict on their relatives," says the London doctor.

Drug addicts lack self-discipline, will-power or ambition and cannot stand pain or any form of discomfort, including criticism or frustration. Addicts become social outcasts and lonely people.

Treatment of narcotic drug addicts must include psychotherapy, says this English physician, and she reports on the use of this approach in combination with the provision of drugs to the patients under the English plan of providing narcotics to addicts in needed dosages. The treatment attempted in this study was first to stabilize the addict on a minimal dose of his needed drug, then after psychiatric treatment directed toward the basic personality problem, to attempt complete withdrawal of the narcotic.

Results of combined treatment of 50 drug addicts are difficult to assess. Dr. Frankau says that nine of 10 Canadian addicts with good cultural and social backgrounds and adequate finances have been freed from drugs for two years or more. Forty other Canadians came to London to avoid trouble in Canada such as prison sentences for delinquency or criminal acts and have not responded so well to the combination of psychotherapy and controlled dosages of drugs. Seventeen are being sustained on heroin, but are able to work. Four patients have failed to report for further treatment. Nine became free of addiction, but one relapsed to the use of heroin. Seven have been convicted of criminal offenses and been imprisoned in London. One patient died.

dreams, the unconscious and hypnosis
in treatment of the heroin addict

Torda, Clara. "An Effective Therapeutic Procedure for the Heroin Addict," Perceptual and Motor Skills, 26: 753–754, June 1968.

A member of the Downstate Medical College of the State University of New York reports on the application of information gained from the patient while falling asleep and the technique of light hypnosis for treatment of 25 heroin addicts to help them resist return to the drug after withdrawal.

Information was gained from the addict while he was falling asleep by means of special equipment that permitted him to awaken sufficiently to answer questions as to what was going on in his mind and to report fragments of dreams. From information of this nature Dr. Torda gained some insight into the pressing problems of the patient and some aspects of his psychopathology, his emotional makeup, defenses, attitudes and thoughts.

Light hypnosis was used to increase the will power of the patient and to decrease his anxiety and depression, as well as to promote good working habits. Posthypnotic suggestions for the addict were based upon the concept of his character structure gained by the psychiatrist from the sleep and dream data. Directive therapy was also used. For example, Dr. Torda told the patients that "from now on you will feel relaxed, worthwhile, strong, and happy. You will feel physically good. You will be able to fall asleep and to wake up ambitious and alert. You will enjoy working."

Over a period of six months readdiction to heroin was significantly reduced or prevented, according to the New York physician. Three patients were given psychotherapy for a longer period of time and have been off heroin for over five years. [No information is given for the other patients.—Ed.]

aversion treatment

Thomson, I. G. and N. H. Rathod. "Aversion Therapy for Heroin Dependence," The Lancet, 2: 382–384, August 17, 1968.

Two English psychiatrists observe that the medical treatment of patients dependent on heroin has given disappointing results and that any treatment that may give better results should be explored.

The Graylingwell Hospital doctors report the use of an aversion treatment based upon statements of some addicts that the ritual of fixing the needle and injecting the heroin is an important part of the process of dependence on the drug. This concept was reinforced in the minds of the psychiatrists when one addict asked for the injection of anything, even water, and another drug user was found injecting himself with tap water.

The aversion treatment consists of the use of a drug (Scoline) timed to produce temporary paralysis and a disagreeable experience at the time of self-injection of heroin repeated over a period of five days. Ten patients were treated in this manner as part of a broader program with encouraging results. The actual procedure consisted of an insertion of a needle into the vein of an addict by an anaesthetist, with a screen to block the addict's view so that he could not see the precise moment of injection of Scoline. The patient is then asked to prepare himself a fix of heroin and to talk about his pleasant experiences with the drug. As he sits on a bed and prepares to inject himself, the anaesthetist, on signal from the psychiatrist, quickly injects the anaesthetic drug. As soon as "paralysis" is imminent the patient is told to inject himself and he then collapses on the bed. Injections can be timed to produce results within one second. As indicated above, treatment is continued for five days.

Ten patients completed the aversion treatment and none used the heroin left with them after each treatment. Eight of the addicts have not used heroin since completion of the treatment, as verified by urine analysis for signs of heroin.

Other parts of the treatment program include withdrawal under methadone, individual and group psychotherapy, self-expression by the addict, occupational therapy, individual and group work with parents, rehabilitation of the addict into the community, close and prolonged followup and repeated urine checks for evidence of drug taking.

With such a complex of treatment procedures it would be difficult to separate effects of the aversion treatment from results that might be due to some of the other therapies. Caution that liver function and hemoglobin levels should be normal and that the aversion treatment should not be undertaken lightly suggest that complications may be possible and that the procedure has limitations. [This report does not give proof of its effectiveness, since aversion is not isolated from other components of the treatment. Any treatment that produces paralysis, even on a temporary basis, would carry some hazard for the patient.—Ed.]

withdrawal at home a failure

Berle, Beatrice Bishop and Marie Nyswander. "Ambulatory Withdrawal Treatment of Heroin Addicts," New York State Journal of Medicine, 64: 1846–1848, July 15, 1964.

Two New York physicians report on their efforts to provide medical care for 268 heroin addicts without putting them into the hospital. The study lasted slightly more than three years and was designed to see if heroin addicts living in a slum area would seek medical and psychiatric help in withdrawing from drugs.

At first, unselected patients were admitted to the neighborhood family clinic without screening. Of 194 drug addicts who sought help only 84 came a second time. After this experience addicts were admitted only if the family and church of the neighborhood agreed.

The withdrawal method of treatment was used and the purpose of treatment was to give relief from withdrawal symptoms. Multiple vitamins were given along with drugs such as meprobamate, chlorpromazine, glutethimide, methylphenidate hydrochloride and chloral hydrate for home use by the heroin addict. In short, the addict himself and his family supervised his use of the drugs at home to ease distress during withdrawal. The foregoing drugs were non-narcotic in nature.

Only 53 patients of the 268 addicts succeeded in withdrawing from heroin. Of these 53 patients 10 were able to stay off heroin for six to 25 months. A followup study of the 53 patients showed that 32 returned to heroin in less than a month and of the others two died of an overdose, one from an intercurrent disease, one was hospitalized, one was imprisoned and 11 relapsed to heroin after two to four months.

Withdrawal treatment entrusted to the addict and his family would thus appear to have been quite unsuccessful.

occupational therapy for the drug addict

Slobetz, F. W. "The Role of Occupational Therapy in Heroin Detoxification," American Journal of Occupational Therapy, 24, 340–342, July–August, 1970.

An occupational therapist of the psychiatry department of the Beth Israel Medical Center in New York described the role of his specialty in the treatment of heroin addicts at the latter hospital.

Craftsmen in painting, ceramics, metalwork, sewing and home economics work in seven shops with modern, professional tools to provide projects that can be completed in a short period of time. The addicts find the shops open seven days a week and they may work in them on a voluntary basis.

One shop is devoted solely to metal work and is aimed at the vocational level. Staff members work closely with patients to evaluate their ability to handle responsibility and to judge whether they can be recommended for employment.

Three primary values for occupational therapy for drug addicts undergoing treatment are judged to be: 1) the ego and self-confidence of the drug user can be strengthened by learning of new skills and completion of projects within a short length of time; 2) nonverbal nature of the therapy makes it possible for some addicts to begin to communicate with others more effectively, and 3) attitudes toward work and employment are improved by completion of projects under the patient's own direction.

The physical therapist proposes occupational therapy as an effective instrument in the psychiatric treatment of drug addicts.

treatment with narcotic antagonists

Fink, Max. "Narcotic Antagonists in Opiate Dependence," Science, 169: 1005–1006, September 4, 1970.

A member of the New York Medical College in New York City says there is a great deal of chaos in the treatment and prevention of heroin addiction.

He believes that narcotic antagonists offer unique opportunities for extinction of opiate-seeking behavior and the conditioning aspects of addiction. Not all narcotic antagonists would be satisfactory for various reasons.

Nalorphine (Nalline) is not a suitable narcotic antagonist for treatment and prevention of addiction because studies show it would have to be injected every three hours to block the effects of morphine given every six hours.

Cyclazocine has been found to protect against both the effects of opiates and the production of dependence. Acceptance of and continued treatment with cyclazocine has been achieved with about 40 per cent of male addicts and some have gone without relapse for more than three years. However, cyclazocine used daily has been found to produce side effects such as irritability, inability to sleep, and illusions. However, the drug appears to have promise.

Naloxone (n-allyl-noroxymorphone) in single injections have been found to be effective against opiates for three to five hours. The absence of side effects indicates promise, but the antagonist needs to be tested more extensively and the cost is high.

Other narcotic antagonists are now being produced and eventually may be used as implants to prevent addiction in high-risk populations, especially in juveniles, according to Dr. Fink. This concept of an "immunization" procedure, he believes, should be tested.

naloxone versus heroin

Fink, Max, Arthur Zaks, Robert Sharoff, Arnoldo Mora, Alfred Bruner, Stephen Levit and Alfred M. Freedman. "Naloxone in Heroin Dependence," Clinical Pharmacology and Therapeutics, 9: 568–577, September–October 1968.

Four physicians and two associates of the New York Medical College report that recent research with narcotic antagonists have given encouraging results in the treatment of heroin addiction.

An antagonist prevents the feeling of well-being that comes from the opiates, helps to control the drug-seeking responses, reduces the risk of developing dependence, and permits the addict to become more interested in rehabilitation.

The short-acting antagonists, such as nalorphine, levallorphan and cyclazocine unfortunately cause many disturbing side effects such as general discomfort, constipation, elation, anxiety, dizziness, agitation, sleeplessness, hallucinations and other reactions. Withdrawal symptoms may occur after cyclazocine.

Naloxone is a more powerful opiate antagonist than nalorphine or levallorphan. In this study seven patients were given naloxone by mouth. They had been using narcotics daily for three to 13 months immediately preceding hospitalization, although they had used narcotics irregularly for four to 17 years. Nineteen other heroin addicts received the latter drug followed by injection of naloxone. Ten other addicts received naloxone by injection before heroin.

The effects of naloxone were shorter than those of heroin. Although the effects of the latter drug began to wane within two minutes after naloxone, they also returned after about three to five hours, indicating the influence of the anti-narcotic was no longer effective. Only minor adverse effects were reported by the patients in this study. Slight depression was reported, but this reaction abated spontaneously or with better adjustment of dosage. Irritability and sensations of temperature change occurred, but these reactions also wore off after a few days of treatment.

The researchers concluded that naloxone by vein is a potent, rapidly acting narcotic antagonist that counters the effects of heroin, but that the latter has a longer duration of action. The absence of serious side effects make naloxone a potentially useful anti-narcotic that may lead to a reduction of drug-seeking behavior of the addict. The high cost of naloxone and the fact that its effects are shorter than those of heroin may be limiting factors in its use.

treatment failures and anti-narcotic
possibilities

Fink, Max, Arthur Zaks, Richard Resnick and Alfred M.
Freedman. "Treatment of Heroin Dependence with Opiate
Antagonists," Current Psychiatric Therapies, 10: 161-170,
1970.

Four physicians of New York report that all forms of treatment of opiate addiction produce discouraging results because of the high rate of addict return to the use of drugs.

The variety and multiplicity of the forms of treatment are
in themselves evidence that all exhibit a high degree of treatment failure, although in some programs the percentage of
failure is reduced somewhat by a careful selection of patients
with high motivation for cure.

Addicts withdrawn from heroin report that they crave the
drug as soon as they return to the community in which their
habit developed and flourished. This association of drug desire and community has caused some psychiatrists to reason
that the high degree of relapse to heroin after treatment is
due to both environmental and physiological conditions.
Blocking of the relief that addicts obtain from heroin might
condition the patient to final extinction of drug-seeking behavior and elimination of physical dependence.

Naloxone is a pure opiate antagonist that may be a suitable drug for blocking the effects of heroin, which conditions
an addict to drug-seeking behavior due to stressful stimuli in
the environment. If heroin can be used repeatedly by the

addict without anticipated effects of relief then it is possible that extinction of drug-seeking behavior may occur. An anti-narcotic, such as cyclazocine or naloxone, may be an effective part of treatment to change the drug-seeking behavior of the addict.

drug treatment of infant addicts

Kahn, Eric J., Lois L. Newmann and Gene-Ann Polk. "The Course of the Heroin Withdrawal Syndrome in Newborn Infants Treated With Phenobarbital or Chlorpromazine," The Journal of Pediatrics, 75: 495–500, September 1969.

Three physicians of the College of Physicians and Surgeons of Columbia University and the New York University School of Medicine observe that although tremors, irritability, watery stools and a shrill cry are the most common symptoms of infants when they are withdrawn from heroin, these signs and symptoms are difficult to assess.

The three doctors report their observations on 38 newborn infants with symptoms due to withdrawal from heroin. Symptoms appeared within the first 24 hours in 28 of the infants. In the remainder the symptoms were observed within 70 hours.

All of the mothers volunteered the information that they were heroin addicts with intakes of one to 45 bags (glassine envelopes containing about five milligrams of heroin mixed with lactose and sometimes quinine) daily.

The three doctors treated the addict babies with pheno-barbital and chlorpromazine with good results. With treatment they felt that withdrawal symptoms from heroin should not be a direct cause of death, and there was only one death in this group of 38 newborn addicts. This death occurred at the age of 1½ months in a baby that had been free of withdrawal symptoms after the age of three days. The baby had apparently been well and the exact cause of death could not be determined since the addict mother refused autopsy permission.

Since an untreated control group of babies was not used in this study the doctors could not tell if the cessation of symptoms was due to the drug treatment. However, they felt that the use of drugs to control discomfort, irritability and other signs is justified in severely affected babies, even if the drugs do not produce a cure in themselves.

heroin maintenance and other treatments

Bewley, Thomas H. "The Diagnosis and Management of Heroin Addiction," The Practitioner, 200: 215-219, February 1968.

A London psychiatrist says there are many treatments for the heroin addict and all have limited successes. In Great Britain the Ministry of Health has recommended that treatment should begin with detoxification (withdrawal) and should then proceed to physical rehabilitation, psychotherapy, occupational therapy, industrial therapy, followup, counseling and advice in various settings such as outpatient clinics or half-way houses and support with a wide variety of sedatives, hypnotics and tranquilizers.

Treatment of withdrawal symptoms usually involves the handling of a craving for drugs, anxiety, restlessness and running of the nose. The symptoms are unpleasant but not usually dangerous.

Rehabilitation is a matter of long-term treatment and involves a complex group of efforts, as described in the first paragraph.

Psychotherapy is needed because drug addicts have other problems with their addictions. Underlying personality defects suggest the heroin addicts have a need for more intensive psychotherapy than is usually available for them.

Group approaches are based on various concepts of self-help and include such organizations as Narcotics Anonymous, Synanon, and Daytop Lodge. The first is modelled after Alcoholics Anonymous, the second is a voluntary organization that sponsors groups of addicts living together and remaining free of drugs, and the third is more of an open community founded by an ex-member of Synanon.

Narcotic antagonists, such as cyclazocine, provide the addict an opportunity to maintain a state of abstinence from heroin or morphine because the antagonist cancels the feeling of euphoria that addicts obtain from heroin.

Methadone has a longer action than heroin and can be substituted for the latter. Methadone is a synthetic narcotic of the opiate type. When given on a daily basis the heroin addict loses his desire to take the latter drug.

Heroin maintenance is the most controversial form of treatment, even in England where it is legal, according to Dr. Bewley. It is still being debated as to whether the supplying of heroin to an addict causes more harm to him and society than if other forms of treatment were used. With heroin prescription no one has yet evaluated whether or not the addict has a good work record, whether he sells part of the drug he gets or gives some to friends and whether or not the addict should be taught aseptic injection techniques in an effort to lower the high death rate. In other words, the full effects of this form of treatment have not been adequately evaluated.

11

methadone

Slightly more than 20 years ago methadone was identified as a narcotic, but only in the last several years has its use been advocated as a substitute for heroin. In 1965 Dole and Nyswander reported that methadone had been used with 22 heroin addicts in the preceding year in conjunction with a rehabilitation program that had succeeded in promotion of return to school, finding of work, and reconciliation with families. Since that date the methadone treatment has been criticized by some physicians and supported by others. The method of treatment is now being used both in hospitals and out-patient clinics under medical supervision and with the provision of social services.

The methadone treatment does not cure the heroin addict. It substitutes another narcotic at a modest financial expense compared to the costs of heroin and it appears to make at least partial rehabilitation more possible. The full effects of this treatment, in which some weaknesses have appeared, remains to be fully established with further research.

the first methadone study

Dole, Vincent P. and Marie Nyswander. "A Medical Treatment for Diacetylmorphine (Heroin) Addiction," Journal of the American Medical Association, 193: 646-650, August 23, 1965.

Two physicians of the Rockefeller Institute and the Beth Israel Hospital in New York City reported the first study of 22 heroin addicts who were treated for one to 15 months with methadone with encouraging results, especially in respect to their social performance and release from heroin.

Disappearance of narcotic hunger for heroin appeared to be the most dramatic result of treatment with methadone, but perhaps the most significant result was related to the patient's ability to return to work and other socially desirable performances. The extent to which the patients ceased to behave as heroin addicts was verified by their own statements and failure to find evidence of drugs in the urine, even though the addicts had ample opportunities to obtain drugs from friends or pushers. The few episodes of drug taking were spontaneously reported by the patients and were verified by urinary findings.

Constipation was the leading complication. No other major ill effects were described by the addicts given methadone. Mental and neuromuscular functions appeared to be undisturbed.

Only two patients were discharged from the study because of uncooperative, disruptive, and psychopathic behaviors.

The investigators concluded that a single daily dose of methadone, taken by mouth, may be an acceptable substitute for heroin in a program of maintenance treatment that might permit addicts to live a normal life. [There are now reports on thousands of such cases. The evidence has been sufficiently convincing in favor of detoxification to encourage numerous programs throughout the country, but some authorities are still skeptical.—Ed.]

methadone treatment raises questions

Ausubel, David P. "The Dole-Nyswander Treatment of Heroin Addiction," Journal of the American Medical Association, 195: 949–950, March 14, 1966.

A physician of the University of Illinois says that treatment of heroin addicts with methadone raises important medical and sociological questions.

Methadone differs from the effects of morphine only in regard to withdrawal symptoms, which are milder. Treatment with methadone merely substitutes the feeling of well-being obtained from heroin for that obtained from methadone, according to Dr. Ausubel.

The Illinois physician says he fails to appreciate how legalized addiction would be any improvement over illicit addiction and thinks the former would be morally less defensible because it indicates that society would be aiding in the personality deterioration and social demoralization that has accompanied narcotic addiction for hundreds of years.

He questions the proof that patients on methadone have been converted to useful and socially productive citizens

when they have been followed in the study for such a short
length of time, with 10 of the 22 cases followed for less than
two months.

The methadone treatment is not directed toward withdrawal but toward the permanent creation of euphoria, says
the physician. He also calls attention to other questionable
conclusions and sees certain potential problems of addiction
that will not be solved by methadone. [The reader is encour-
aged to investigate more recent reports by this author to
compare the results of five-year follow-up studies with this
report.—Ed.]

seventy-nine patients treated with methadone

*Dole, Vincent P. and Marie E. Nyswander. "Rehabilitation of
Heroin Addicts After Blockade With Methadone," New York
State Journal of Medicine, 66: 2011-2017, August 1, 1966.*

Two New York physicians, the country's leading research
workers on the value of methadone in the treatment of heroin addicts, report their observations and results with 79 of
the latter who had been under treatment for three months
or longer.

First, the doctors make the point that medical research
must find the solution to heroin addiction, because putting
addicts in jail does not solve the problem. On release almost
all addicts go back to their drugs. Law enforcement is

necessary, however, to control the illegal traffic in heroin and to protect against property damage and loss.

The crucial test of any treatment lies in the ability of the addict to resist drugs when he returns to the community and to accept the responsibilities of attending school, going to work, and functioning well in society. As matters now stand, each heroin addict in New York City costs the community about $25,000 per year in addition to many indirect costs that involve welfare, hospitalization, unemployment, losses of property, increases in insurance costs and overhead expenses and other factors. Although this report covers only 79 addicts, a total of 107 were being treated with methadone by the New York doctors, and they calculate that even with this small number of heroin addicts who have gone off the drug, the community has been saved three million dollars, due to the reduction of drug-related crime, reduction of costs for hospitals and jails and removal of families from welfare as the addicts become reemployed.

The methadone treatment, at the time of this report, began with a six-weeks hospitalization, during which time small doses of oral methadone were prescribed, with a gradual raising of the dosage to a blockade level for heroin. The program was not a locked-ward treatment. Patients were permitted to leave to visit families, go to work, go to school, shopping or engage in other out-of-hospital activities. No formal psychotherapy or group sessions were used.

Methadone has been found to be very safe, with no damage to general health or nutrition, liver, kidney, bone marrow or neuromuscular functions. No medical problem caused by methadone developed in this study. Addicts have accepted the treatment. They have not diverted the medication into illicit channels, and urine tests have verified that the addicts are staying off heroin.

Seventy-one per cent of the 79 addicts have made social adjustments such as finding work, attending school, keeping house, engaging in useful social activities and cessation of criminal activities. The program failed for 11 per cent who were discharged for psychopathic behavior even though they had ceased taking heroin. Each of these patients tried to regain admission into the program.

methadone blockade treatment

Nyswander, Marie and Vincent P. Dole. "The Present Status of Methadone Blockade Treatment," American Journal of Psychiatry, 123: 1441–1442, May 1967.

Doctors Nyswander and Dole report that heroin addiction can be stopped with methadone, but that effective social help must also be given to the addict for his social problems remain after he has ceased using heroin.

The physicians report that a three-year study involving more than 200 patient-years of medical and behavioral information has shown methadone programs to be consistently able to stop heroin addiction.

The cost of the methadone blocking treatment, including data collection, social services and counseling is approximately $2,000 per patient for the first year and is about $1,000 each year thereafter. This cost is less than one-fifth of the cost of confining an addict in a hospital, and the effectiveness is far greater than that of any other medical program, say the two physicians.

276 heroin addicts on methadone reveal
heroin addiction as a metabolic disease

Dole, Vincent P. and Marie E. Nyswander. "Heroin Addiction—A Metabolic Disease," Archives of Internal Medicine, 120: 19-24, July 1967.

The two primary research scientists on methadone versus heroin indicate that because no specific psychotherapy has been used in the treatment of 276 heroin users (except for some individual counseling) in the methadone program at Beth Israel Medical Center, that heroin addiction should be considered as a metabolic disease. This concept is in keeping with psychiatric studies that fail to reveal an "addictive personality," say the physicians.

Moralists often believe that heroin is a pleasant drug that can be resisted by strength of character, but the fact that methadone produces a physiological blocking of the pleasant effects of heroin indicates that the problem is biological in nature. For most normal persons heroin is not enjoyable in the initial exposures.

No comparable success in the treatment of heroin addicts to that of methadone has been achieved by psychotherapy, believe the doctors. This fact casts some doubt on the psychogenic theory of the origin of addiction to heroin, but does not disprove it. The doctors acknowledge that basic character defects may lead persons to addiction after which metabolic changes occur that make the drug habit a metabolic problem.

The New York physicians report that 276 heroin addicts who have been treated with methadone are now living socially acceptable lives and that many more street addicts are now waiting to enter the program of treatment and rehabilitation. Whether or not the patients are different is no longer a practical issue, but the theoretical question remains as to whether methadone maintenance masks the symptoms of an addictive personality.

The unexpectedly favorable response of heroin addicts to a methadone maintenance program has caused the doctors to reexamine the psychogenic theory of addiction. New evidence suggests that the traits and characteristics of heroin addicts are a consequence of addiction rather than a cause of the latter. The fact that substantial numbers of addicts can be rehabilitated on a medical program suggests that heroin addiction is essentially a metabolic disease, not a psychogenic one. [Another authority states that conclusion suggested here is not necessarily adopted by himself or others.—Ed.]

methadone rehabilitation without a cure

Walsh, John. "Methadone and Heroin Addiction: Rehabilitation Without a 'Cure'", Science, 168: 684-686 (No. 3932), May 8, 1970.

A member of the American Association for the Advancement of Science observes that efforts to rehabilitate heroin addicts have been discouraging, but in recent years treatment with the synthetic pain reliever methadone has given practical help to large numbers of heroin users. Methadone involves the substitution of one narcotic for another, so there is confusion as to how laws against one can be reconciled with laws permitting the other.

Methadone treatment, especially in New York City, has caused addicts to stop using heroin, to return to school or work, and to modify the antisocial behavior that is characteristic of addicts. If methadone is stopped it is expected the addict will return to heroin. Thus, methadone offers rehabilitation without a cure.

Methadone is legally approved and used rather widely for two major purposes: 1) as a pain killer, and 2) for detoxifying or withdrawing heroin addicts. The drug is readily obtainable by physicians who use it for these two purposes. The current problem arises because the use of methadone in long-term treatment programs legally is a "new use" for the drug and its safety and value must be established by the Food and Drug Administration before it can be used on a broad scale.

When obtained legally the cost of a daily dose of methadone for one person is about that of a cup of coffee, but the total costs of an effective methadone treatment program are between $1,500 to $2,000 per year.

In New York detailed records on about 2,000 persons treated with methadone are available in a computerized data center. A urinalysis procedure is used to detect any return to the use of heroin and detection of barbiturates in the system is now possible also. The New York program also provides medical examinations and treatment for other illnesses, job and education advice and supportive counseling. These services explain why the cost of methadone treatment exceeds that of just the drug alone.

Success is judged to have been achieved when the addict gives up heroin, and lives a life that is free of crime and other antisocial behaviors. The program has been successful for 82 per cent of all the addicts accepted into the treatment plan, according to reports.

Critics of the methadone treatment plan point out that it does not work for persons using other drugs, that some heroin addicts use it to reduce their tolerance to heroin so that they can resume the use of the latter drug at a lower dosage, and that if provided for young people who are not heroin addicts that they will be made into methadone addicts.

There are now about 60 research investigations going on with methadone and others are planned. The FDA is not yet satisfied of its safety and value as of the date of this report.

methadone treatment of 750 criminal addicts

Dole, Vincent P., Marie E. Nyswander and Alan Warner. "Successful Treatment of 750 Criminal Addicts," Journal of the American Medical Association, 206: 2708–2711 (No. 12), December 16, 1968.

Two physicians and a research associate report the results of a four-year trial of methadone in the treatment of 750 criminals addicted to heroin.

By 1965 it was believed by the investigators that heroin addiction could be treated with methadone hydrochloride which blocks the action of heroin and erases the compulsive desire for heroin. Tolerance to methadone develops with daily doses of the drug given by mouth. The treatment program was divided into three parts, the first of which included six weeks of hospitalization during which time the proper dosage of methadone was determined so that blockage of heroin occurred. Now, favorable results are being obtained through an outpatient clinic without hospitalization. The second part of the treatment began when the patients were discharged from the hospital but reported daily for their methadone except for weekends when medication was given to take home. At the clinic a urine specimen was taken on each visit for analysis and the addict was required to swallow methadone at least once a week to demonstrate that he was maintaining his tolerance by taking the drug daily. Part three of the treatment began when the patient had become a stable and socially productive member of the community, after which he was treated as a regular medical patient.

Some patients, when freed of heroin addiction, have stopped all antisocial activity, have found jobs, and have begun to support their families. Usually, however, the slum-born, minority group, criminal addicts needed vocational training, and other social assistance.

Prior to treatment with methadone 91 per cent of the patients had been in jail. The 750 heroin addicts had a record of about 4,500 convictions, but for every conviction the usual addict had committed hundreds of criminal acts for which he was not apprehended. Approximately 94 per cent have been free of criminal offenses since completion of the methadone treatment. Reduction of crime was judged to be at least 90 per cent by the investigators. All patients convicted of crime and removed from treatment by imprisonment were discharged from the methadone treatment.

Blockade by methadone makes heroin relatively ineffective, so that it does not provide a feeling of well being and withdrawal symptoms do not develop, but some patients may be tempted to return to heroin because they may remain drug-oriented in their thinking. However, urine analysis done three times per week for one year revealed no evidence of self-administered narcotics in 55 per cent. About 15 per cent of the patients continued to use heroin intermittently. The greatest surprise of the methadone treatment has been the high rate of social productivity as measured by stable employment and responsible behavior.

medical evaluation of the methadone treatment

Methadone Maintenance Evaluation Committee. "Progress Report of Evaluation of Methadone Maintenance Treatment Program as of March 31, 1968," Journal of the American Medical Association, 206: 2712-2714 (No. 12), December 16, 1968.

The Evaluation Unit of the Columbia University School of Public Health and Administrative Medicine, with Henry Brill, M.D. as chairman, has been given the task of judging the outcome of the treatment of hardcore heroin users with methadone. The Committee makes the following observations, based upon the records of 544 men:

1 The patients being treated with methadone were all well-established heroin addicts for an average of 10 years addiction.

2 The average age was 33 years, with a range of 20 to 50 years.

3 Sixty-eight per cent of the patients were over 30 years of age.

4 Forty-eight per cent of the addicts were white.

5 Approximately one-half of the addicts did not finish high school.

6 Practically all of the addicts have well-documented histories of repeated arrests, jail terms, and treatment failures, before beginning the methadone treatment.

7   All of the patients entered the program voluntarily.

8   During hospitalization, during the first part of the treatment, the patients were given a great deal of personal, social, and psychological support, as well as necessary medical and dental care.

9   Physicians, social workers, nurses, counselors and former addicts being maintained on methadone all played an essential role in the support given the addicts.

10   During the second phase of treatment, when the patient was supplied with medication for several days at a time and returned twice a week to the clinic for urine testing, the major emphasis was given to helping him get a job, return to school, and increase skills by taking technical training.

At the beginning of treatment only 28 per cent were employed, but after 24 months of methadone treatment 85 per cent were employed or in school. At the start of treatment 40 per cent were on welfare, but only 15 per cent after two years. None of the patients who have continued under care have become readdicted to heroin, although 11 per cent have been found to use amphetamines or barbiturates repeatedly and about five per cent have chronic problems with alcohol.

The Committee judges the methadone program as a successful one, but points out the group is older, is voluntary, and may be more highly motivated. Nevertheless the Committee recommends expansion of the program, extension to other groups such as young addicts and prison inmates, further research and continued follow-up and evaluation of the results over a longer time. [The reader might wish to investigate Committee reports for 1969, 1970 and 1971.—Ed.]

methadone and criminal behavior of addicts

Dole, Vincent P., J. Waymond Robinson, John Orraca, Edward Towns, Paul Searcy and Eric Caine. "Methadone Treatment of Randomly Selected Criminal Addicts," The New England Journal of Medicine, 280: 1372–1375, June 19, 1969.

Two physicians and four research associates report a study of the effects of methadone on the criminal behavior of heroin addicts with records of five or more jail sentences and who were in prison at the time of the beginning of treatment.

Seventy per cent of 165 prison inmates applied for the methadone treatment after a single interview. Eighteen of the inmates were randomly selected for methadone treatment with imminent release dates. Treatment of these prisoners was started before they left jail. An untreated control group of 16 prisoners was used for comparison.

That motivation for relief from heroin can be induced was shown in this study in which it was shown that desire for relief increases in a series of steps, as follows: 1) a willingness to listen about a new treatment program; 2) requests for more information; 3) continuation of interest; 4) application for treatment, and 5) persistence in treatment after admission to the program.

The Rikers Island prison, in which this study evolved, contained approximately 1,500 heroin addicts with known criminal records. Addicts chosen for the study were selected by lottery from a group soon to be discharged from prison.

Methadone treatment was started 10 days before discharge and continued thereafter under medical guidance.

Results of the study, seven to 10 months after release from prison, showed that all of the untreated men became readdicted to heroin, whereas none of the treated group became regular daily users within that length of time. One-half of the methadone-treated group was employed or in school, and showed no more convictions for criminal acts. Six patients with the best results are living as responsible members of the community and supporting their families.

If the results of this study can be applied to the total prison population of criminal heroin addicts then it should be possible to transform approximately 5,000 dangerously antisocial prisoner addicts into acceptable citizens by treatment with methadone, say the six members of the research team.

progress report on methadone

Blachly, P. H. "Progress Report on the Methadone Blockade Treatment of Heroin Addicts in Portland," Northwest Medicine, 69: 172-176, March 1970.

A physician of the University of Oregon Medical School in Portland says the goal of methadone treatment is not cure of addiction, but the removal of criminal activity on the part of heroin and other drug addicts.

The doctor reports his own experience with the methadone treatment after observing that treatment failures with other methods have ranged from 70 per cent to 99 per cent.

Dr. Blachly reports that methadone is able to suppress the withdrawal symptoms of heroin abstinence for 18 to 36 hours. The methadone treatment is based on the theory that in some people heroin produces metabolic changes in which the craving for drugs is so great that the addict will engage in any criminal activity to get the narcotic. Thus, methadone treatment permits the addiction to continue, but removes its social and physical evils, according to Dr. Blachly.

At the time of this report the Portland physician had about 75 heroin addicts in a methadone treatment program. He began treatment with four addicts in prison one week before they were to be discharged. All four of these heroin users are now stabilized, employed, and paying taxes. Two addicts still in jail, but who are released on work-release permits, are also being treated. None of the 75 heroin users on methadone are receiving any formal psychotherapy. Most have had extensive psychiatric treatment elsewhere.

The doctor sees the patients once a week, in the beginning, and adjusts the dosage of methadone as necessary. Prescriptions for methadone must be presented daily to one pharmacy and the drug must be consumed on the premises. It cannot be taken away for sale or giving to other addicts. Once the patients are stabilized for methadone dosage the physician sees them every three months. The few failures to date have been with persons using other drugs simultaneously, especially of the barbiturate and tranquilizer types.

Dr. Blachly has found that an acetylmethadol compound (a synthetic cogener of methadone) works for 72 to 96 hours compared to the 18 to 36 hours for methadone, and he is now in process of trying to work out a research program regarding its effectiveness with heroin addicts. In the meantime he believes that the methadone program in Portland is successful in terms of social rehabilitation and decrease in crime so far as heroin addicts are concerned.

methadone versus acetylmethadols

Jaffe, Jerome H., Charles R. Schuster, Beth B. Smith and Paul H. Blachley. "Comparison of Acetylmethadol and Methadone in the Treatment of Long-Term Heroin Users," Journal of the American Medical Association, 211: 1834-1836, March 16, 1970.

Two physicians and two associates of Illinois and Oregon report that the necessity of taking methadone every 24 hours causes some problems for heroin addicts because the daily travel needs to visit a clinic may be difficult, especially if they are employed and have reassumed family obligations. Reliable patients may be given extra supplies of methadone for home use, but with some addicts there is the possibility that the anti-narcotic may be sold or accidentally consumed by non-addicts in whom the effects might be quite serious.

Acetylmethadol compounds can prevent withdrawal symptoms for 72 hours or more, in contrast to about 24 hours for methadone, although it has a common action.

Twenty-one volunteer patients who had been stabilized on methadone were instructed to take the new form of methadone. Twelve of the patients were assigned to the experimental group and nine to the control group. For seven weeks the patients had to report to the clinic only three times a week instead of six or seven times. On each visit they were tested for opiates in the urine and a symptom list to judge the severity of any withdrawal symptoms. Sixteen of the addicts completed the study.

Although the acetylmethadol compound was taken only three times a week, former compulsive heroin users who had made satisfactory social adjustments on methadone continued to do as well on the new anti-narcotic. Heroin withdrawal symptoms were effectively suppressed for 72 hours.

Four patients dropped out of the study because of undesirable side effects from the acetylmethadol compound. Anxiety and confusion occurred in some of the patients, but may have been psychogenic in origin. However, those patients who did not experience side reactions were more comfortable on the new drug treatment and were reluctant to return to methadone.

Acetylmethadol compounds may have advantages over methadone in the treatment of heroin addicts. The possibility of side reactions needs more study.

acetylmethadol and methadone

Editorial. "Methadone and Acetylmethadol," Journal of the American Medical Association, 211: 1847–1848, March 16, 1970.

An editorial in the Journal of the American Medical Association observes that a significant step forward in the treatment of heroin-dependent persons may have been achieved in the preceding report by Jaffe and his associates. One of the most troublesome aspects of the methadone treatment is that the patients must take the drug every day by travelling to a clinic or other source, or else be given an extended supply of the drug which may lead to abuses, including illegal sales in the street.

Some of the basic questions that still need to be answered are whether or not the hard-core street addict can be motivated to enter programs of this kind and whether they will respond to counseling and other social services for long-term rehabilitation. Also unresolved is a fundamental ethical question as to whether or not it is proper to perpetuate a person's drug dependence by substituting methadone or acetylmethadol for heroin for an indefinite time.

problems, questions, and limitations

of methadone treatment

Torrens, Paul R. "Methadone Maintenance Treatment Program," Hospitals, 44: 76–81, December 1, 1970.

In a presentation at the New School for Social Research in New York City, a physician who had experience for three years with a methadone treatment program at St. Luke's Hospital Center, stated that of 2,205 heroin addicts only 18 per cent were lost to the program for one reason or another.

An amazingly high rate of success was obtained, says Dr. Torrens, and of the addicts still in the program from 75 to 90 per cent are employed, in school, or are full time homemakers.

Of the heroin addicts who did not complete the methadone treatment most were lost to the program because of alcoholism, problems with the law, non-heroin drug abuse and medical or emotional problems not related to heroin.

Questions and problems still remain even though the methadone maintenance program has been successful, according to this physician. One question is that since methadone is a narcotic itself, isn't the patient's addiction merely being shifted from one drug to another? Differences between the two drugs are great, however. Heroin must be injected, methadone can be taken by mouth. Heroin has serious side effects and interferes with the patient's ability to function normally. With methadone the patient can make an adequate social adjustment. It is said by some persons that methadone creates its own "high," but a committee of the American Medical Association reports that it does not have any notable effect on mood or consciousness. Other criticisms have been made, such as methadone is a way to keep minority groups down, but the reality is that heroin addicts will never withdraw from heroin without something like methadone. It is heroin that keeps certain minority groups down, whereas methadone frees them to return to school, work, and families. Methadone programs have been criticized because they do not prevent drug addiction, but many of the heroin addicts who have been freed by methadone become most active in prevention efforts. Some critics have said it is the counseling and psychological support that is given the methadone patient that produces the real success, but there is evidence that without methadone there would be no effective counseling or psychological support. Methadone appears to make the latter possible. It has been rumored that methadone has unusual and harmful side effects, but thorough investigation shows these effects are minor and time and treatment cause them to disappear. It is said that addicts who leave the methadone treatment return to heroin; so does this fact not prove that methadone is not a cure? It is true that methadone protects persons from addiction so they can function normally in society. Whether they will eventually be cured of addiction to heroin only time can tell.

moral, ethical, and medical considerations

Kramer, John C. "Methadone Maintenance for Opiate Dependence," California Medicine, 113: 6–11, December 1970.

A member of the medical faculty of the California College of Medicine at Irvine, in commenting on the effectiveness of methadone in controlling the heroin addict's craving for his drug, his daily injections, his illegal activities and in promoting a return to the ordinary activities of living, also observes that the morality of prescribing a narcotic for maintenance has been challenged.

When the physician prescribes methadone is he guilty of an immoral act? No, says Dr. Kramer, for if a specific treatment brings substantial benefits to the patient it can be accepted as a logical and desirable treatment until something better is found.

Medical provision of insulin for diabetic patients, anticonvulsive medicine for epileptics, or antipsychotic agents for the mentally ill person has long been accepted as a legitimate and moral act on the part of the physician.

The California physician reports that six years of methadone treatments have been carried out in about 50 programs with approximately 10,000 patients and that results have been good. Dr. Kramer gives effective answers to a number of questions and criticisms regarding the methadone treatment and concludes that most of the moral, ethical, and medical objections that have been raised against it are groundless.

"Potential savings to the community . . . of addict-caused crime . . . the costs of law enforcement and incarceration are vast. The value of the salvage of tens of thousands of lives, the restoration of addicts to their communities, their families and themselves, cannot be measured," says the physician.

methadone for outpatients

Moffett, Arthur D., Walter R. Cuskey and William F. Wieland. "Utilizing Methadone in Outpatient Treatment of Narcotic Addicts," Clinical Medicine, 78: 29–36 (No. 3), March 1971.

The Program Director of the Narcotic Addict Rehabilitation Program and two associates of Philadelphia describe an outpatient methadone treatment program in that city.

The report covers 300 methadone patients in treatment at the time of this report although a larger number were in the program. Addicts were admitted to treatment if they were on narcotics, wanted the treatment, and lived within the area. Most referrals came from informal communications on the street with addicts in the treatment program or from the

Philadelphia General Hospital. A few came by referral from physicians or social agencies.

At first the addicts had to report to the clinic six days a week. On each visit the patient was counseled by a professionally trained person or an ex-addict who was off heroin and had received special training. Some patients received in-depth psychotherapy. Methadone dosage was gradually increased to a stabilizing level.

Originally the addicts were hospitalized for six to eight weeks for methadone stabilization and other phases of the beginning program. Shortage of hospital space and experienced personnel led to the establishment of the outpatient program with equally good results. Complications occurred in only about 15 per cent of the patients and diminished or disappeared as tolerance to methadone developed. Complications included constipation, delayed menstruation, obesity, ankle swelling, nausea and impotence in men. Constipation was the most common side effect.

Seventy per cent of the addicts were under the age of 20 years when they first became addicted. At time of treatment heroin was the drug most frequently used with an average of slightly more than eight years history of addiction. About 95 per cent of the addicts had at least one criminal conviction and about one-fourth had been treated before for addiction.

At first about 60 per cent of the patients on methadone will cheat and use other drugs, but with testing of the urine on each visit and with further methadone treatment cheating diminished to about 30 per cent after 20 months. However, of the 30 per cent who cheated only about 15 per cent of that group gave evidence of heroin usage in the urine tests.

With methadone treatment on an outpatient basis approximately 64 per cent of the patients were able to hold a job and about 95 per cent were no longer being arrested. Salaries of the working addicts ranged from $100 to $1,200 per month with an average of $275. The Philadelphia group considered it to be of prime importance that under the outpatient approach rehabilitation occurred in the community with its normal stresses. Some patients would accept treatment only on an outpatient basis as they did not want to be hospitalized. Outpatient treatment was found to be much cheaper than hospitalization, costing about $1,300 per year. This amount would cover only about one month in the hospital. The group recommends the outpatient methadone treatment for heroin addicts.

recommendations for methadone treatments

"Methadone Maintenance Techniques," California Medicine, 114: 62-63, June 1971.

Committees of the American Medical Association and the National Research Council have issued a joint statement of recommendations on the use of methadone maintenance in the treatment of narcotic addiction, as follows.

1 Methadone treatment should provide for supervised urine testing for detection of morphine and other drugs, should have adequate facilities, general medical and psychiatric services, hospital facilities as needed, an adequate staff and rigid controls to prevent illicit sales of the drug or its intravenous use.

2 Patients should not be selected who have not been on heroin but who now become dependent on methadone.

3 Long-term evaluation of patients should be continued. [Another authority adds that such evaluation should be extramural and independent.—Ed.]

4 Staff members should be trained in methadone programs that have been found to be effective.

5 Continued research is particularly important.

The joint statement indicates that methadone maintenance is not feasible in the office practice of private physicians because they cannot provide all of the needed services or meet all of the treatment needs of the patient. The private physician, in the opinion of the committees, cannot guarantee the addict will keep the drug out of illicit channels, cannot maintain control of doses or provide adequate evaluation of results. They can, however, cooperate with methadone maintenance programs in their communities by providing services they are capable of rendering.

methadone poisoning of children

Aronow, Regine, Shashi D. Paul and Paul V. Woolley. "Childhood Poisoning An Unfortunate Consequence of Methadone Availability," Journal of the American Medical Association, 219: 321–324, January 17, 1972.

Three physicians of the Department of Pediatrics of Wayne State University School of Medicine observe that in the widespread acceptance of methadone as a substitute for heroin in the addict, little attention has been given to the danger of methadone for small children.

Within nine months of the opening of a methadone substitution clinic in Detroit, 18 cases of accidental swallowing of the drug came to medical attention because of serious reactions on the part of the children, including death in one instance. An additional 23 cases of methadone poisoning of children occurred in the following seven months, so it is apparent that the drug is hazardous for children. Although the lethal dose of methadone is thought to be about 75 milligrams for adults and that 60 mg. could be fatal for a child, the experience and observations of these physicians is that as little as 10 to 20 milligrams of methadone may prove fatal. In this study the children were mostly in the age group of one to three years. Parents, other relatives, and baby sitters were the primary sources from which the children obtained the methadone.

Serious depression of breathing is the most dangerous and toxic effect for children and this difficulty in respiration may last up to 48 hours, even with treatment. Symptoms of methadone poisoning of children included drowsiness, coma, temporary cessation of breathing, shallow respirations, sleepiness and stupor, although in two cases none of the foregoing signs were present. Small, constricted pupils were present in all except two of the children.

The physicians discuss treatment which is primarily directed to the maintenance of respiration, proper use of fluids, removel of unabsorbed drug and other measures such as the use of nalorphine.

Delay in getting the methadone-poisoned child to medical care seems to be related primarily to total unawareness of parents to any danger from methadone until drowsiness and difficulty in breathing was apparent.

As higher dosages of methadone become available, especially from illegal sources on the street, it can be expected that the hazards to children will increase, the three physicians believe.

12

multiple responsibilities

The use of narcotic drugs has relationships to personality problems of the individual, legislation, education, legal counsel, law enforcement, judicial interpretation, recreational facilities and programs, medical effects and other components of a very complex nature.

Heroin is a drug that can temporarily alleviate the stresses and pains of humanity, which is unfortunate because society must face its problems as individuals or groups, rather than evade them with drugs. The problem of crime and heroin has not been solved to-date. The social significance of the methadone treatment of heroin addicts lies in the fact that provision of the former drug may alleviate the burden of crime in a community burdened by the costs of addiction as reflected in shoplifting, stealing, robbery and other forms of crime from which the heroin addict raises money.

No consideration of the problems created by the widespread use of heroin can be adequate without observations on international aspects. The growing and marketing of opium, from which morphine and heroin are made, is done outside the boundaries of the United States. The manufacture of heroin from these products is done abroad. The finished product is smuggled into this country and sold on the illicit market. So long as international cooperation in control of heroin is lacking the burdens of suppression of the heroin trade rest with us. The need for effective diplomatic leadership on the international scale should be obvious.

costs to society of 81 heroin addicts

Cushman, Paul. "Methadone Maintenance in Hard-Core Criminal Addicts," New York State Journal of Medicine, 71: 1768-1774, July 15, 1971.

A physician of the St. Luke's Hospital Center in New York City observes that chronic addiction to heroin is one of the major medical, social, and economic problems of the present.

In this study the criminal activities of 81 heroin addicts attending the Methadone Maintenance Clinic are reported. The primary sources of funds for obtaining heroin were usually multiple in number, and included the following; welfare, selling drugs, stealing, work, prostitution, family, pimping, begging, gifts, forgery on checks, going into debt, pickpocketing, purse snatching and use of savings. The number of days spent in jail during one year before methadone was 1,931. No time was spent in jail after the addicts began to be treated with methadone. The 81 addicts also spent 346 days in detention prior to methadone treatment.

An estimate of the cost to society of these 81 heroin addicts prior to the beginning of methadone treatment was calculated from information gained from the addicts and the known costs of materials stolen, service rendered, and so on. The average daily cost of heroin for the group was $34.85, but the daily range was from $0 to $150. During the prior year the 81 addicts raised $887,800 from selling drugs, stealing, prostitution, forging checks and pimping. The fair market value of stolen goods was estimated to be $721,000 for the single year. Other costs to society included approximately $23,800 for welfare, $67,260 for detoxification treatment of the 81 addicts in a hospital, $12,000 for treatment of other drug-related illnesses, $28,230 for costs of keeping the addicts in jail, $4,150 expenses for days in detention and $900 of expense involved in arrests of the addicts. Since all of the foregoing costs involve only one year in time and the small number of 81 heroin addicts, it should be clear that for the nation as a whole drug addiction must constitute a fantastic financial burden.

Improvement after methadone treatment was spectacular and spared society in New York City alone hundreds of thousands of dollars, and violent crimes committed by the group ceased. As Dr. Cushman expresses it: "Expensive, violent, and criminal while using heroin, the patients change significantly after methadone. Some individuals become strikingly positive influences in society."

drug addiction and legal responsibility

Armstrong, John D. "Responsibility and Addiction," Canadian Psychiatric Association Journal, 11: 116–122, February 1966.

The Medical Director of the Addiction Research Foundation and member of the Department of Psychiatry at the University of Toronto observes that a common concept in law is that ordinary or natural man or reasonable man, intends the natural consequences of his acts. He is presumed to be able to understand and predict these results and therefore to be responsible for them.

Concepts are changing. Now it is recognized that many factors influence a person's responsibilities for his acts. Now questions are being asked and especially so in the field of drug usage.

Many laws pertaining to the manufacture, sale and use of drugs may bring a person into conflict with the law. Greater legal problems occur when drug-induced behaviors occur that are not acceptable to the community or to society at large. Many laws are inconsistent in respect to their actual significance. A person, for example, convicted of possession of a narcotic drug may be sentenced to from seven years to life, whereas a drunken driver who endangers the lives of others may draw a much lighter sentence.

Behaviors are influenced by many factors that may change or impair abilities and powers of decision. Traffic laws may stress impairment of driving ability as a hazard to society and emphasis has been placed on alcohol as a major problem. However, driving capacity may be impaired by fatigue, hunger, an acute illness, a chronic disease, an emotional disturbance involving anger, frustration, despair, anxiety or elation. Mental competence and stability of temperament may be involved. And so may drugs, as well as many other factors.

Drug addiction involves a process whereby a person comes to have less and less control over his own behavior, says Dr. Armstrong, and thus the responsibility for his behavior comes into question. As addiction develops the addict may find himself going into situations where he is likely to get involved in damage to others, whereas in pre-addiction days he would not have gotten into such occurrences. Is he more or less responsible under the influence of drugs?

Degrees of responsibility exist. There are degrees of predictability and probability. Serious physical or mental disorders, depression or other factors may be related to the drug abuser's acts, so that responsibility for an act may not be attributed solely to addiction. The degree of responsibility is especially important when punishment is involved. Communities may have greater responsibilities for examining the abilities of people as they change with drugs.

policies toward heroin addiction

"Contradictions in Addiction," Public Health Reports, 78: 669-672, August 1963.

A conference on narcotics held at the University of California in Los Angeles brought out that policies toward addicts are shared by law, custom, and public opinion rather than by physicians or persons responsible for the treatment of criminals.

Treatment of addicts in custody, in a hospital or an institution of correction, tends to impose its own rules of iron necessity in order to keep drugs out of the hands of addicts and to limit unauthorized departures from the treatment program. "Even if addiction is not regarded as a crime, it is difficult for the addict to avoid punishing experiences."

juvenile courts and the drug problem

Goldberg, Marion. "Problem of Drug Abuse in Juvenile Court Population," New York State Journal of Medicine, 71: 1623-1626, July 1, 1971.

The Supervising Probation Officer of the Courts of New York City says it is the juvenile term of the Family Court that has jurisdiction over a broad range of issues involving young people. The Probation Service is often asked to make investigations for the court and administers the Juvenile Center for young people who must be detained.

A rapid increase of drug addiction among young people has been observed during the three years preceding this report. Heroin was found to be the leading drug being abused, followed by marijuana. In a one-month period 72 per cent of the children referred to probation were using heroin. In this same month during 1969 it was found that 10 per cent were sniffing glue and only three per cent were using marijuana among those who were sent to the probation officers. It is quite likely that marijuana users alone would not be referred.

The typical child who goes through a court process and is then referred to probation as a drug user has been found to be poor in a family that lives on marginal income or public assistance. He is disorganized, often with one missing parent, has made poor school adjustments and has limited recreational outlets. He tends to live from day to day.

Programs and facilities available to this age group of drug addicts are virtually non-existent, according to the probation officer. Confrontation techniques often used with older

addicts do not appear to be appropriate for the younger addicts. When committed, these young children are treated as
part of the total, older population. An urgent need exists for
specially-designed programs involving residential care for this
age group, says the probation expert.

law enforcement is not enough

*Larkworthy, Frank R. "Aspects of Law Enforcement in Drug
Control," American Association of Industrial Nurses Journal,
15: 7–10, August 1967.*

A Supervisory Agent of the U.S. Food and Drug Administration Bureau of Drug Abuse Control in Los Angeles points out
that there are three ways in which the Federal government
can help cope with the drug abuse problem. These three ways
are: 1) prevention; 2) education, and 3) enforcement.

Without drugs of abuse there would be no abuse, says the
Food and Drug expert. The distribution of dangerous drugs
needs to be controlled. On the other hand, the enlightened
public is less likely to react to drugs as though they are harmless, if the true nature of drugs is known. Thus, a program of
education is needed to remove as much as possible the ignorance which surrounds drug abuse. An enforcement program
is needed to control the peddlers and others who make drugs
available. Law enforcement alone is not enough to stop an
illegal traffic in drugs, but it is worthwhile if it helps to take
some of the profit out of the drug trafficking.

ineffective health laws on drug abuse

Curran, William J. "Public Health and the Law: Dangerous Drug Abuse: Three Stories on a June Day," American Journal of Public Health, 61: 1445–1446, July 1971.

A Professor of Legal Medicine of the faculty of Public Health and Medicine at Harvard University says that ineffective health laws regarding drug abuse exist at the local, national and international levels.

To illustrate his point he calls attention to three news reports that appeared in the *New York Times* on June 3, 1971. He believes these three stories give the most compelling evidence of the growing problems of drug abuse that he has seen in one place.

The first story told of the deaths of two people from a heroin overdose on the steps of a New York hospital. The young man was 22 years old and the girl was only 16. Several weeks earlier the girl's older brother, aged 20, had also died of an overdose of heroin. These two deaths were the 423rd and 424th deaths from dangerous drugs in New York City in a period of barely more than five months in 1971. One of the comments made without rancor or ill will was that these kids are "a bunch of idiots. They don't know what they're doing and now they are dead."

The second story in the same newspaper concerned a federal court conviction of a 65-year old doctor in Manhattan for running a "supermarket" in amphetamines in his office. Patients came from as far away as Texas to receive his "speed shots." Many former patients testified against the doctor. The conviction was the first in a new drive against doctors in large cities who are alleged to be making fortunes on drugs. The judge sentenced the physician to five years in prison and a $10,000 fine.

The third story involved a report on testimony before a Congressional committee in which it was stated that 80 per cent of the heroin coming into the United States is grown in Turkey. Most of the rest comes from Burma, Thailand, and Laos. The governments of these countries are said to be directly involved in growing the opium poppy, manufacturing heroin and distributing it under ineffective international controls.

More effective laws are needed at all levels to combat the modern-day epidemic of drug abuse, says Professor Curran.

medical viewpoints slow court decisions

Morgan, Robert. "Drugs: A Court or Medical Problem?" The Health Bulletin, 85: 10–11, October 1970.

The Attorney General of North Carolina observes that courts are being overwhelmed with cases involving drug addiction. Of 300 cases of narcotic violations in that state many are more than two years old.

Doctors, psychologists and social workers are becoming more insistent that drug cases be treated from the medical standpoint rather than from a punitive approach. One result of this growing attitude is the inability of the courts to insure a speedy trial or to compel medical treatment and rehabilitation for the defendants.

Lack of flexibility in sentencing makes it almost impossible for courts to deal with drug abuse from the medical viewpoint. Existing narcotic laws rigidly define the sentences for each offense and they often make any medical considerations impractical.

The attorney general says it is clear that combined efforts of law enforcement agencies, the courts, correctional facilities, specialized treatment resources and a more rapid administration of justice for more effective control of drug abuse problems are needed.

responsibility for drug treatment
returning to the physician

"Methadone vs. the Evils of Narcotics Addiction," Medical Tribune, 7: 7ff. (Section I), March 26–27, 1966.

Dr. Conan Kornetsky of Boston University School of Medicine observed in a symposium of medical experts on the subject of narcotic addiction that the medical profession "abdicated its responsibility for this problem 40 years ago and turned it over to the law enforcement people. Hopefully it is now returning to the physician."

The Boston physician also observed that alcoholism is a greater problem than opiate addiction but that the latter is regarded as criminal behavior while alcoholism is considered a sickness.

medical prescription of drugs in a
canadian city

Cooperstock, Ruth and Mary Sims. "Mood-Modifying Drugs Prescribed in a Canadian City: Hidden Problems," American Journal of Public Health, 61: 1007–1016, May 1971.

Two research associates of the Addiction Research Foundation of Toronto, Canada report a study of drugs prescribed by physicians in that city. The study was concerned only with the consumption of drugs, not their misuse, abuse, addiction or other problems. Only the mood-modifying drugs were studied, and it was found that these products accounted for 24 per cent of all prescriptions that were issued.

In a single year, based on the samples studied, it was calculated that 1,369,000 prescriptions were issued in this one city. Since there were 1,351,000 persons over the age of 15 years, the investigators concluded that about one mood-modifying prescription was issued for all adults in the space of one year. Of course, the investigators observe, a small part of the total population may have accounted for all the prescriptions. From their data, however, the researchers believed that every day of the year seven people out of every 100 are taking a mood-modifying drug.

Only eight per cent of the prescriptions were filled in the hospitals; 92 per cent were dispensed by retail pharmacies.

Sedative and hypnotic drugs accounted for 44 per cent of the prescriptions, with antidepressants and tranquilizers a close second and accounting for 40 per cent of the total. Other drugs, mostly amphetamines, accounted for 16 per cent of the prescriptions. The sedatives used were predominantly barbiturates alone or in combination. Librium and phenobarbital were the drugs most often prescribed by physicians. However, 26 different drugs accounted for about 80 per cent of all the mood-modifying prescriptions.

Seventy per cent of the prescriptions were written by general practitioners, with psychiatrists accounting for about five per cent of the prescriptions. Since psychiatrists represent about five per cent of the medical profession in the city, they did not appear to be writing prescriptions excessively for the mood-modifying drugs. Physicians who graduated after 1960 appear to be more cautious about prescribing the drugs in question.

when is a drug safe to use?

Dews, Peter B. "The Pharmacologist's Dilemma: When is a Drug Safe for General Consumption?" Pediatrics, 45: 3–6, January 1970.

A psychobiologist of the Harvard Medical School raises the question as to when a drug is safe for general consumption.

Heroin can cause a rapid development of tolerance and physical dependence. Getting and injecting heroin at regular intervals becomes a way of life. The heroin habit replaces normal physiological and social conduct and results in what may be called a malignant addiction.

Heroin seems to be free of any direct damage to the liver, lungs, kidneys, bone marrow and so on in ordinary doses, but frequently kills people when an overdosage is obtained, as may so easily happen.

The Harvard faculty member observes that some people contend that anyone should have the freedom to go his own way, but points out that the climate of our society today is different. People expect to take care of their neighbors and expect the government to help.

hospitals have responsibilities

Rooen, Will. "Hospitals Responsible for Alcohol and Drug Addicts," Canadian Hospital, 47: 5-6 (No. 2), February 1970.

The editor of *Canadian Hospital* observes that drug addicts and alcoholics have created such problems of conduct during hospitalization that many staff members are reluctant to admit them, but he believes that changes in attitudes must occur.

The hospital is becoming more and more the center of community health care and the public especially looks to the hospital for emergency care. In this hospital specialist's viewpoint hospitals should serve as the emergency unit for alcohol and drug cases. "The first seven days are critical in alcohol and drug withdrawal and the hospital has the medical and nursing facilities to deal with them."

This Canadian authority observes that crash pads and emergency units are coming into being and creating another layer of health services in the community without proper medical supervision. For legal and other reasons the hospital is often avoided in preference for these resources on the part of the addict.

In Canada several provinces are approaching the problem constructively and hospital associations are beginning to establish guidelines for greater service to drug addicts, especially during emergency periods.

group psychotherapy for heroin addicts

by a community of laymen

Myers, Kenneth. "Heroin Dependence: A Community Experiment in Therapeutics," The Lancet, 1: 805–806, April 13, 1968.

A staff member of the Fulbourn Hospital in Cambridge, England says the poor results of present treatments of heroin addicts should encourage other approaches.

In this report a description is given of a community program of weekly, two-hour meetings of an informal nature where heroin addicts can keep in touch with the ordinary, adult society they are in danger of rejecting completely.

Discussions at the meetings can be on any topic, but usually center around attitudes of families and society and problems of work. Specific requests for help that are made by any addict are always fully discussed by the total group and an attempt is made to render the help requested.

Members of the group include the addicts and the helpers. The helpers include physicians, theology students, teachers, housewives and other segments of the total society. The total group acts as a forum for airing grievances, criticisms of society, requests for help and as a channel of communication for explaining national and local policies on drug abuse. Many of the helpers find themselves defending society, but find themselves torn by the impossibility of meeting unrealistic demands by the heroin addicts for work, shelter, heroin and other services. Gradually the helpers find themselves accepted by the addicts and they in turn find they have often forged the first link in the chain of rehabilitation, says Dr. Myers.

No claims are made for this form of group psychotherapy, but it gives the heroin addict two hours a week to discuss personal problems with some remote chance that he may gain insight into his difficulties. Laymen in the community have an opportunity to become better informed about the problems of the heroin addict and to keep alive a link between the latter and the community in which he lives.

a crisis-intervention center in a
suburban-rural area

Denison, John M. "An Unusual Social Experiment to Help Youth in Crisis," Canadian Medical Association Journal, 104: 15-19, January 9, 1971.

The Clinical Director of a Crisis Intervention Center reports on this service to young people in Newmarket, Ontario in Canada. Although so-called "crash pads" or intervention centers are now well known in big cities, this report concerns the operation of a center in a suburban-rural area covering an area of about 20 miles and run by young people to help other young people.

Early discussions and investigations among 2,500 young people revealed that drug experimentation was widespread among high school youth and extending down into grades seven to 10. It was felt that no single arm of the community could solve the problem of growing drug abuse and that it was a "whole community task," although there was severe community inertia.

Social action committees were formed composed of both youth and adults. Key resource people in the community were identified. Educators, police, medical and paramedical personnel and a base was established from which young people could operate as a team of workers.

A pilot plan was rapidly inaugurated to give honest, factual information, to discourage the use of hard drugs, to provide a place to which young people could relate and come to with trust and confidence, and to help, when asked, in any crisis situation. Housing was found, financial support was raised, and a staff was formed of young people who knew the drug scene well and who were concerned and experienced in handling "life-situations." A professor, two college students, three grade 13 students, and two young married men comprised the final staff that was chosen. Volunteer helpers, an administrator and a family doctor to serve as clinical director were also linked with the service. The purpose was to offer a 24-hour service to youth in crisis. The word chosen for the organization was Ankh, Egyptian for "life."

The majority of clients are now handled by staff members directly without the need of further professional aid, although medical or other help is occasionally needed. About 50 per cent of the clients do not have drug problems, but come with various personal difficulties, such as quarrels with parents, being thrown out of home, being out of work, being worried about pregnancy or venereal disease or just to sit and think for awhile. In a typical weekend about 130 young people will visit the service. Of these about 30 will have acute drug problems such as an overdose of "speed," reactions to drug impurities, bad trips, and so on. One night 17 young people telephoned to discuss drugs they were taking. Young people like the service because of the warm understanding staff, the comfortable old house, the presence of animal pets, the guarantee of anonymity, and the cooperation of various agencies that otherwise keep "hands off."

The service is far less costly than other procedures and is believed to be more effective by staff members. Future plans call for more counseling and education, establishment of a "job-bank," possibilities of establishing a "half-way" house, getting more volunteers and other activities.

synanon and rehabilitation of the drug addict

Batiste, Curt G. and Lewis Yablonsky. "Synanon: A Thera-peutic Life Style," California Medicine, 114: 90-94, May 1971.

A psychiatrist and sociologist collaborate on a description of Synanon as a controversial community program for the treatment and rehabilitation of narcotic addicts.

The Synanon program is described as a much broader one than the curing of drug addiction; changes in life styles are advocated based upon group therapy, racial integration, a different form of religion and a fresh approach to cultural arts and philosophy. The organization is proposed as a vehicle for constructive personal and social change.

Many of the people who come to Synanon have not been addicted to drugs, but come seeking a new life style. Drug addicts with criminal records find themselves living with people from all walks of life.

The game is the most widely used group process. Several times each week all members participate in an intimate group reaction in which fears, problems, hostilities and other emotions can be expressed freely. Participants can be creative, spontaneous, rigid, angry, loud, or passive as they choose. Only physical violence is prohibited.

Therapeutic characteristics for drug abusers are identified as: 1) involvement; 2) an achievable status system; 3) a new social role; 4) flexibility and social change; 5) social growth; 6) social control, and 7) empathy and self-identity.

[It is difficult to say how effective the above measures may be in helping the drug addict, as the authors provide only a description of Synanon activities and concepts rather than research proof of its effectiveness.—Ed.]

united states a primary target for

heroin smugglers

"U.S.A. is Promised Land of Global Drug Peddlers," Medical Tribune, Page 8, February 26-27, 1966.

Interpol (International Criminal Police Organization) reported to the United Nations Commission on Narcotic Drugs that the United States is the main target for narcotics smugglers and that heroin is the primary drug in this illicit traffic, despite the fact that this country does not have the greatest proportion of drug addicts in terms of population.

The United Nations Commission reports that nations with one narcotic addict per 1,000 of the population or less include the Congo, South Africa, Bolivia, Peru, Iraq, United Arab Republic, Cambodia, Nationalist China, Hong Kong, Macao, Malaysia, Pakistan, Singapore and Thailand.

It is estimated that the United States has one addict for every 1,000 to 5,000 persons. Other large countries of the world in this category include Brazil, Canada, Mexico, India and Japan.

In Europe, at the time of this report, all the countries were estimated to have less than one addict per 5,000 persons. [The heroin addiction rate in Europe has changed for the worse since the date of this report.—Ed.]

federal action against drug addiction

"New U.S. Agency Begins Drug War," American Medical News, Page 1, August 23, 1971.

A Special Action Office for Drug Abuse Prevention has been established by the President of the United States to restore public confidence in drug abuse prevention and rehabilitation programs, to bring scattered programs together in a coordinated effort, and in general to gain control over the rising tide of drug addiction in this country.

Doctor Jerome Jaffe, a Chicago psychiatrist, has been appointed as head of this agency. One of his first moves was to go to South Vietnam to set up more effective control measures over the use of heroin through a urinalysis screening and detection program.

Nine different federal agencies are currently involved with some phase of drug abuse prevention and plans call for the linking together of their various activities into a better coordinated effort. The new office will not take over these agencies, but will have strong influence in respect to policies that guide the programs.

The methadone maintenance program of treating heroin addicts will receive a great deal of attention and will be combined with psycho-social counseling and rehabilitation. Leadership of the American Medical Association is looked for and it is expected that this organization will guide the government in proper medical practices in connection with drug abuse.

Returning servicemen will probably be subjected to a 30-day detention period if traces of opiates are found by urine screening techniques, providing legislation pending in Congress at the time of this report is approved. The Veterans-Administration hospitals for drug treatments will be increased from five to 32 in the near future if plans crystallize.

Drug addiction has been called "Public Enemy Number 1" by President Nixon and the establishment of the special action office is one of his first moves against the problem. The office has been established for a period of three years, but can be extended for a longer time if necessary.

the british system of treating heroin addicts

heroin addicts

Edwards, Griffith. "The British Approach to the Treatment of Heroin Addiction," The Lancet, 1: 768-772, April 12, 1969.

A member of the Addiction Research Unit of the Institute of Psychiatry in London says the British system of treating the heroin addict also aims at prevention of the spread of addiction and is based on the concept that the drug addict is a sick person rather than a criminal.

Prior to 1968 any English doctor could supply narcotics to any patient in any amounts providing he kept proper records. He even had no obligation to supply authorities with the number of drug addicts that he might be treating.

The Dangerous Drugs Regulations of 1968 came into operation on February 22nd of that year. This new law specifies that unless they are given for the relief of pain due to organic disease or injury, heroin and cocaine can be prescribed only by doctors who have special licenses. A license is good only at new special centers for drug addiction, mostly in teaching hospitals. Any doctor seeing an addict must now report in written form this information within seven days.

Dr. Edwards contends that the new law is not adequate in some respects and that it may have difficulties from persons who are not addicts but who demand to be registered as and treated as heroin users; from conservative prescribing on the part of physicians who cannot judge accurately the precise needs of an addict; from persons who use the black market to obtain heroin because they do not want to register with the government; from difficulties in building motivation on the part of addicts to come off heroin; from decisions that must be made for compulsory admission to hospitals and determination of just when an addict is stabilized.

Whether Britain "at a time of many transitions is a country which can make the system work remains to be seen," says Dr. Edwards.

can school authorities search student

lockers for drugs?

Hudgins, Jr., H. C. "Locker Searches and the Law," Today's Education, 60: 30–32, November 1971.

An Associate Professor of Temple University who is an authority on the legal aspects of public school activities reports that although a rash of civil liberties cases has challenged school regulation of student behavior since 1960, the courts have in general sustained the right and responsibility of school personnel in measures designed to safeguard the health and safety of pupils and school personnel.

The courts have not answered specifically whether or not teachers can conduct locker searches for drugs or other substances, but the student cannot deny entry to school administrators, according to Professor Hudgins. Thus, it is wise for teachers to avoid locker searches and to let the school administrators conduct them.

Policemen may search student lockers in schools when they are armed with a warrant, but the courts have not clearly indicated if they may conduct such searches without a warrant. A general search may be made without a warrant, as in the event of a bomb scare (in which case the police search all lockers looking for a reported bomb). It appears wise, however, for a policeman to have a warrant if he singles out one particular locker for a drug search.

The California Appeals Court has held to the position that the power of the state to control the conduct of children (students) is greater than its authority over adults.

Students do not own their lockers. They are held by boards of education in trust for the state. The student does, however, have some control over his locker. He may, for example, keep other students from having access to it. The courts permit school administrators to search lockers, but they should be prudent in doing so. It is wise for the administrator to have a third party present as a witness. The student should be present when the locker search is made, but he should not be warned in advance because he may destroy evidence. He should be informed of the search while the administrator is accompanying him to the locker to open it, in the presence of a witness. Prior student consent is not needed, although better relationships may be maintained if it is requested. The search can be made anyway. One court has held that the school official's right to conduct a locker search "becomes a duty when suspicion arises that something of an illegal nature may be secreted there." The Fourth Amendment prohibits only "unreasonable search and seizure" . . . thus a reasonable search would be implied if school authorities have reason to believe the student's locker contains something detrimental.

index